ENTERTAINING
PEOPLE

✦

MENUS FROM A PACIFIC NORTHWEST
COOKING SCHOOL

———————

BY
DAN & KATHLEEN TAGGART
GEORGIA VARELDZIS
DIANE MORGAN
AUDREY LIEBERMAN

Designed by
PATRICIA ZAHLER

Photography by
JERRY LAROCCA

Illustrations by
JOANNE RADMILOVICH

Edited by
DAN TAGGART

PUBLISHED BY ENTERTAINING PEOPLE
PORTLAND, OREGON
1989

Dedication

We dedicate this book to our students. They encouraged us, sometimes applauded us, frequently overlooked our failings, and probably taught us as much as we taught them.

It is also dedicated to you, gentle reader, in the hope that you will use it often. May your time in the kitchen be entertaining and fun! Best Wishes.

ISBN 0-9620937-0-X

Published by Entertaining People
17080 SW Arkenstone Dr.
Durham, Oregon 97224

Printed in Korea through Codra Enterprises

ACKNOWLEDGEMENTS

If you find our book appealing it is because of the efforts of several people who deserve mention. All of them have made a significant contribution; some of them provided critical services.

Marianne Barber. Kathleen's sister in Chicago tested more recipes than any other single person outside the authors' group. Her mailed comments reflected the honest advice we needed from a non-author tester.

Patricia Zahler. She is responsible for the beautiful design and layout of the book. She spent countless hours readying designs without any assurance that the book would ever really happen.

Jerry LaRocca. Jerry photographed the food and the authors. He is a perfectionist and we learned a great deal about good photography just by watching him work.

Betty Shenberger. Betty not only tested recipes and passed out moral support but also lent the beautiful quilt used for the picnic photograph. If Betty pronounces your food good, it's good.

Louise Poust. Many of the antique props used in the photographs were kindly lent by Louise. If you are planning a book and need antiques talk to Louise. She has a house full!

Dick Schuettge. We began our project as rank amateurs. We needed advice about how to proceed. Dick was kind enough to take on a consulting role and helped guide us through the maze of details.

Martie Cobb. Martie has typed and re-typed more than she ever dreamed possible. If typos are found, they are attributable to our lack of proof-reading skills, not to her lack of diligence.

The Cooking School Staff. Betty, Louise, Nancy, Shannon and all the others--most especially Karen-- gave support in so many ways for so long. They all are good friends who have happily eaten rejects more than once, and cleaned up after our late night cooking sessions.

TABLE OF CONTENTS

No member of this small band of cooks was trained as an entertainer, so far as we can tell. And yet, beginning in the late 1970's and very early 1980's, there occurred a series of events which were to change the way each member of our group thought about the word "entertainer." One by one, probably beginning with Georgia, each innocent cook found himself standing at a range in the corner of a retail kitchenware store. The range was enshrouded by a large, round, wooden table at which were seated as many as 30 men and women intent on learning the secrets of good cooking--at least, those secrets pertaining to the menu of the evening. The cook--losing innocence rapidly--discovered that not only was he expected to produce good food for the consumption of the class but that those quiet moments spent, say, sautéing onions at home seemed more like a deafening silence when spent under the gaze of an audience of adults who had *paid* for the privilege of watching someone cook! Suddenly the broadcaster's phrase "Dead Air" took on a new and quite personal meaning. The cook discovered that it is simply not enough to cook the onions, that he also needed to be entertaining! So the long pauses which naturally result from so many cooking ventures came to be peppered with little asides, comments that may or may not have had much to do with the food at hand. And over the course of two, three, or four hours a menu came together if the cook was lucky, glued together by both cooking skill and a little newfound storytelling ability.

The entertaining was occasionally at the expense of the cook. As a group we must have proved the truth of Murphy's Law beyond a shadow of a doubt: "If it can go wrong it will, and at the worst possible time!" Dan can still remember adding baking soda to an acidic lemon cake batter without including the flour; the resulting eruption from the top of the food processor he was using brought back clear memories of the mudpots at Yellowstone National Park. Diane stared fate in the eye during a pizza class one night. It must have had something to do with trying to shake an unbaked pizza from a wooden "peel" onto a blazing hot pizza stone in the oven. The scene the following morning when Dan opened the oven door was reminiscent of the inside of a backyard incinerator which was legal in decades past! Audrey's demise--at least the one Dan was present to witness--came in the form of a homemade mayonnaise which simply would not emulsify. The softly-peaked emulsion she expected looked like nothing, so much as a separated vinegar and oil dressing decorated with little drops of egg yolk. She survived to sauté another day. So did Kathleen after she liberally coated the inside of a freshly baked tart crust with dijon mustard--a technique commonly employed to help seal the crust against future sogginess. The subtle mustard flavor it imparts is quite appealing in savory quiches and tarts. It did not go particularly well with the sweet peach dessert tart she was demonstrating! Georgia once found herself in the midst of a full-participation class needing only one pound of phyllo dough to supply the students with their raw material. The paper-thin sheets in the first box she opened were torn and stuck together, making their use nearly impossible. Only after opening six boxes was she able to supply the equivalent of one pound of dough! The business of teaching a cooking class is fraught with danger and the entertaining is often at the cook's expense.

We learned more than a few things during those teaching years, especially that there are very few absolutes about cooking. Five cooks can usually find five different ways to produce the same type of food, a fact which made for some lively discussions during the recipe testing of this book. We also learned that people often want menus, not just recipes. Many good cooks find planning an appealing menu harder than the actual cooking. So after years of being asked "When are you going to write a cookbook?" we decided to do just that. The menus in *Entertaining People* are just our ideas of some interesting combinations, nothing more. We have tested the food and found it pleasing, but many of the dishes could be mated in several other ways. See the list of other suggested menus near the end of the book.

Our recipes are our own, for the most part, personally developed but influenced by the other four cooks in the group. (Offering one's food for public consideration--or do we mean dissection--can be a remarkably humbling experience.) Like all cooks, we have been influenced by those around us. We have had considerable opportunity to rub shoulders with some of the most influential cooking authors in America. A partial list of those who have influenced us the most includes: Madeleine Kamman, Anne Willan, Paula Wolfert, Perla Meyers, Maida Heatter, Helen Witty, Bert Greene, Barbara Tropp, Martin Yan, Ken Hom, Hugh Carpenter, Bernard Clayton Jr., Biba Caggiano, Nina Simonds, Jack Lirio, Giuliano Bugialli and Julee Rosso. We learned, also, from the writings of James Beard and Julia Child. They had a lot to do with awakening an interest in good food within several of us.

We learned something else, too, about culinary reality. Classes built around a theme of "light," "low calorie," "good for you" or "low fat" foods simply were not popular. No matter how many requests we received for these kinds of classes, the response, when actually offered, was always nil. So we learned that people may want or need to control their diets in various ways, but when it comes to entertaining, they generally prefer richer menus to "lighter" ones. Since this is a book of menus for entertaining, we have made no effort to control your diet! We firmly believe in the advice offered by Madeleine Kamman about certain kinds of foods, when she says, "Cook it infrequently but cook it right!" We use unsalted butter, exuberantly; cream, because it tastes good; chicken and even duck fat for their incomparable flavors; and at least once or twice several of these in combination. We mean for the food to taste good; you are in charge of adjusting your eating pattern in a sensible way so that you can have your cake and eat it, too!

These are foods for entertaining people. They taste good, we think; you may find ways to make them even better. Your interest and ability in the kitchen will determine how much of each menu you want to tackle. We will admit right here that help gratefully accepted from friends can make several of these menus much quicker to produce. So pass out the assignments, set the dates--and the table--and, most of all, enjoy the eating. Because life is too short for dull food!

Dan Taggart

Kathleen Taggart

Georgia M. Vareldzis

Diane J. Morgan

Audrey Robinson

Gnocchi
Manzo Alla Lombarda (Beef Roast Braised in Wine)
Faglioni Al Burro (Green Beans with Butter and Cheese)
Insalata Mista
Sicilian Cassata

CARNIVALE

arnivale is that wonderful and joyous celebration which happens just before the somber and penitential season of Lent begins. Here in the United States we call it Mardi Gras; in most of Europe it is known as Carnivale! Here we offer a festive Italian party menu, served Italian style--that is, in courses.

First served is the Gnocchi, made with semolina, laced with butter and parmesan cheese. If you can find it buy the real thing--Parmigiano Reggiano. You will be rewarded with the world's best flavor. Our main course is a spicy beef roast braised in red Barolo wine accompanied by simple but elegant green beans tossed with butter and cheese. As is sometimes done in France the salad is served by itself after the main course. Finally, "i dolci"--a decadent, delicious Cassata!! It is pound or sponge cake filled with ricotta, candied fruits, nuts and chocolate. The mocha buttercream--and I do mean *butter*cream--literally melts in your mouth!!!

We would accompany this meal with more of the Barolo wine used for braising the beef, or a good quality Oregon or California Pinot Noir.

Georgia M. Vareldzis

These gnocchi are a sort of baked dumpling, for lack of a better description! They are not difficult to make, but are REALLY good eating!

To serve 6 to 8:

3 cups milk

1 teaspoon salt

3/4 cup semolina flour (available in some supermarkets and many health-food or nutrition centers)

2 eggs

1 cup grated parmesan cheese, divided

4 tablespoons unsalted butter, melted

Freshly ground pepper

Freshly grated nutmeg

GNOCCHI

In a heavy-bottomed saucepan bring the milk and seasonings to a boil over medium heat. Add the semolina gradually, stirring constantly, keeping the milk at a boil--otherwise it will get lumpy! Cook and stir until the mixture becomes very thick. A spoon should stand up unsupported in the middle of the pan. Remove from the heat.

Beat the eggs lightly and add 3/4 cup of the parmesan cheese. Stir it into the semolina mixture. Spread smoothly onto a buttered jelly roll pan (about 10x15 inches). It should be smooth and about 1/4-inch thick. Refrigerate until firm, about 1 to 2 hours.

Preheat the oven to 400º. Butter a shallow baking dish, about 9x9 or a 10 to 12-inch round. Using a 1 1/2 inch round cutter cut the gnocchi into circles. Layer in the baking dish, overlapping slightly. Drizzle with the melted butter and top with the remaining cheese. Bake for 15 minutes until they are crisp and brown. If they do not brown well you can place them under the broiler briefly to finish.

Serve immediately!

To serve 6 to 8:

2 cloves garlic, finely minced

1 teaspoon dried oregano

Salt and freshly ground pepper

8 thin slices Pancetta (Italian bacon, unsmoked), cut into narrow strips

4-5 pound sirloin tip roast

2 tablespoons butter, divided

2 tablespoons olive oil, divided

1 medium onion, chopped

1 carrot, chopped

1 rib celery with leaves, chopped

1 cup dry red wine (Barolo is traditional)

1 16-ounce can whole peeled tomatoes, drained and chopped, juice discarded or used for another purpose

1 bay leaf

1 cup beef or other stock

MANZO ALLA LOMBARDA
(Beef Roast Braised in Wine)

If you cannot find Pancetta, use regular smoked bacon, but blanch it in boiling water for 5 minutes to remove some of its smoke flavor.

Mix the garlic, oregano, salt and pepper together. (If you are using canned broth or bouillon cubes go very easy on the salt at this point!) Toss the seasonings with the bacon strips.

Make deep incisions all around the roast using a thin, sharp knife such as a boning or filet knife. Insert pieces of the bacon in the incisions.

Preheat oven to 350º.

In a heavy oven-proof braising pan heat 1 tablespoon each of the butter and olive oil. Brown the roast well on all sides. Remove from the pan and add the remaining butter and olive oil if needed.

Sauté the onion, carrot and celery for about 10 minutes until they are soft. Using a slotted spoon remove the vegetables from the pan and pour out most of the fat.

With the pan on the heat pour in the wine and deglaze the pan by stirring and scraping up the browned fragments. Reduce the wine to 1/2 cup. Add the cooked vegetables and place the roast on top of them. Add the tomatoes, bay leaf and stock. Bring to a boil. Cover and place in a 350º oven to continue cooking for about 2 hours. Cook until the meat is fork tender.

When the meat is tender remove it to a carving board, cover with foil for a few minutes to rest, then slice.

Strain the cooking liquid into a bowl. Skim off the fat and cook over high heat to reduce and thicken the sauce. I like to purée the vegetables until smooth, then add them to the sauce. Taste and adjust seasonings, if necessary.

Pour some sauce over the meat and pass the remainder in a gravy boat.

To serve 6 to 8:

1 1/2 pounds fresh green beans (use frozen if necessary)

4 tablespoons butter

1/2 cup freshly grated parmesan cheese

Salt and freshly ground black pepper, to taste

FAGLIONI AL BURRO
(Green Beans with Butter and Cheese)

Clean the beans and cook in boiling salted water until crisp-tender. Drain.

Melt the butter in a large skillet. When it foams add the drained beans and cook 2 to 3 minutes over medium heat. Do not break the beans while stirring them. Toss gently with the cheese and remove to a serving plate. Serve immediately.

To serve 6 to 8:

1 large sweet red pepper

1 head romaine lettuce

2 cups sliced fennel bulb (or celery if necessary)

2 medium tomatoes, cut into wedges

1 cucumber, sliced

4 tablespoons olive oil

1 tablespoon Balsamic vinegar (or other good quality red wine vinegar)

Salt and freshly ground black pepper, to taste

Several large, fresh basil leaves

INSALATA MISTA

The sweet red pepper may be used raw, but for better flavor blacken the skin over a flame or under a broiler. Place in a plastic bag for 5 to 10 minutes, then scrape skin off with a paring knife. Remove the stem and seeds, then julienne.

Clean the romaine, dry it and tear into bite-size pieces. Add the remaining vegetables. Pour olive oil, then vinegar and salt and pepper over the salad. Toss to mix, then taste. Add more salt, pepper or vinegar if you wish. Chop the basil leaves very fine, add to the salad, toss again and serve. This salad is nice served after the main course, as a refreshing buffer between entrée and dessert!

SICILIAN CASSATA

To serve 8:

CAKE

1 fresh loaf cake, 9x5 inches

1 pound ricotta cheese

2 tablespoons whipping cream

4 tablespoons superfine sugar

2 tablespoons Strega (an orange-flavored liqueur) or Grand Marnier

4 tablespoons chopped, candied fruit such as cherries and pineapple

2 tablespoons finely chopped pistachio nuts

2 ounces semisweet chocolate, coarsely chopped

FROSTING

12 ounces semisweet chocolate

1/2 cup strong black coffee

2 sticks (8 ounces) unsalted butter, cut into 1/2 inch pieces

For this dessert you may use either a pound or a sponge cake. I have used both from time to time. It needs to be in a loaf shape, however.

Using a sharp serrated knife slice the ends off the cake and slice it *horizontally* into 1/2 inch thick slabs.

In a food processor or mixer combine the ricotta, cream, sugar, and liqueur until they are smooth. Stir in the candied fruits, nuts and 2 ounces of chocolate.

Place the bottom layer of the cake on a serving platter and spread generously with the cheese mixture. Place another cake layer on top and repeat until all the cake and filling has been used. Leave the top piece of cake plain. Press together gently and refrigerate until the ricotta mixture is firm, about 2 hours.

Meanwhile, melt the 12 ounces of chocolate with the coffee over low heat while stirring, until the chocolate has melted completely. Remove from the heat and place in the bowl of an electric mixer. Beat in the butter, one piece at a time, and continue beating until the frosting is smooth. Chill to a spreading consistency.

Using an icing spatula spread the frosting over the top and sides of the cassata. Some of the frosting should be left. Refrigerate both the cake and reserved frosting for about 15 minutes. Then, using a pastry bag and star tip, decorate the cassata. Rose buds and vines are traditional! Cover loosely with wax paper and refrigerate overnight. It is best when refrigerated 24 hours. Slice and serve.

Mayeritsa
Stuffed Roast Leg of Lamb with Roast Potatoes
Sparagia Me Kasseri--Steamed Asparagus with Kasseri Cheese
Horiatiki Salata--Greek Vegetable Salad
Tsourekia--Greek Sweet Bread
Phoenika Yemista--Greek Stuffed Honey Cookies
Kourambiedes--Greek Butter Cookies

GREEK EASTER

It is Easter Eve, midnight in any Greek Orthodox Church, here or in Greece, and the faithful wait in hushed silence in the completely darkened church, holding an unlit candle. Suddenly, behind the closed altar doors, the priest strikes a flame and joyfully announces--"Christos Anesti--Christ is Risen!!!!" The altar boys carry the light to the first rows of parishioners to light their candles, and the light is passed quickly throughout the whole church while joyous, triumphant hymns are sung. After the Liturgy, parishioners return to their homes carrying their lighted candle to grace their tables. Family and friends gather for a supper of soup, sweet bread, cheese, olives and to crack red Easter eggs end to end to see whose will not break. The lamb is killed and cleaned ready to be barbecued whole on the morrow.

This menu is adapted for an American kitchen. Traditionally, the soup is made from the insides of the lamb, but ours is made from the bones only. While some families still roast the lamb whole, most will cook only legs or shoulders. This soup is made with egg and lemon as thickening agents and is quite delicate. Because of this it is very easy to have the eggs curdle. If one is not careful, it can look like egg-drop soup instead!!! The broth has only rice or orzo, a rice pasta, and fresh dill. The boned leg of lamb is stuffed with a seasoned spinach and cheese mixture and is roasted until it is tender and well done. No respectable Greek would be caught dead eating rare or even medium rare lamb!!!!! Potatoes cooked in the lamb drippings are *absolutely* delicious. Burnt butter is used often in Greek cooking and it imparts an entirely new flavor. Here we use it over steamed asparagus along with grated Kasseri cheese. Green beans are also delicious served this way.

The bread, or Tsourekia, is a rich, sweet dough that is braided with red eggs interwoven in the braid. Greek Easter eggs are *always* red, symbolizing the blood of Christ shed on the Cross. There is a great deal of religious significance in Greek food, and the Greek diet is tied directly to the church calendar with its feasts and fasts. Even those who have only a nodding acquaintance with the Church follow these customs.

Of course, the Greek Easter table is laden with sweets (desserts) of all kinds, including baklava. The two cookies given here are my favorites. The kourabiedes, completely covered with powdered sugar, are very traditional. The phoenika, with their secret "surprise" of ground nuts and dipped in thinned honey, are typically Greek in flavors--cinnamon, orange, honey, nuts--absolutely a wonderful combination, I think you will agree!!!!! The kourabiedes can be frozen, but you will need to sift fresh powdered sugar over them when you serve them. Do this after they are defrosted. The phoenika can also be frozen but before they are dipped. The honey will make them fall apart if you dip, then freeze, them. Defrost them and be sure the honey is warm. These cookies are always served in white paper baking cups (the kind you use for muffins and cupcakes).

Kali Orexi!!!!! Good appetite. Kalo Pascha!!!!! Happy Easter.

Georgia M. Vareldzis

MAYERITSA

Cover the lamb bones with water--about 6 to 8 cups--and bring to a boil. Skim off the scum which forms. Add the onion or leek, celery, parsley and bay leaf. Simmer for 2 hours. Strain the solids from the broth and remove most of the fat. This may be done ahead of time.

About 30 minutes before serving time heat the broth to a boil. Add the orzo or rice and simmer for 15 minutes or until tender. Remove from the burner. Let cool for 10 minutes.

Beat the egg whites until they are stiff. Blend in the yolks, lemon juice and water. *Slowly* add some of the hot broth to the egg mixture until it is quite warm. Pour everything back into the pot, stirring constantly. *Do not allow to boil!* Add the dill and serve immediately.

This can be reheated in the top of a double boiler or in a microwave but never directly on the heat because it will curdle.

Lamb bones from the boned roast of the main course

1 large onion or the split and washed white portion of a leek

1 rib celery with leaves

A sprig or two of parsley

1 bay leaf

1/2 to 1 cup orzo (rice-shaped pasta) or long grain rice

6 eggs, separated

Juice of 2 lemons

2 tablespoons cold water

1 tablespoon fresh dill (dry may be used, but it is not as good)

STUFFED ROAST LEG OF LAMB WITH ROAST POTATOES

Cut slits in the lamb and insert the cloves of garlic. Rub the salt and pepper over the meat. Combine the other marinade ingredients and pour over the lamb. Cover and refrigerate overnight.

Make the stuffing by washing and draining the spinach. If you are using frozen spinach thaw it and squeeze all excess moisture out of it. Set aside.

In a sauté pan heat the oil and butter until it foams, then add the pine nuts and shallots and cook until the nuts are golden-colored. Add the spinach and wilt it, cooking slowly until all moisture has disappeared from the spinach. Turn off the heat and add the rest of the ingredients. Cool until you can handle the mixture.

5 to 6 pound boned leg of lamb, fat removed, bones reserved (or use shoulder, though the leg is traditional)

8 to 10 cloves of garlic, peeled

A little salt and freshly ground black pepper

MARINADE

Juice of 1 lemon

1/2 cup red or rosé wine

1/4 cup olive oil

About 2 teaspoons chopped fresh oregano, or 3/4 teaspoon dried

About 2 teaspoons chopped fresh mint, or 3/4 teaspoon dried

1 bay leaf

STUFFING

1 pound fresh spinach, or 1 10-ounce package frozen, thawed

2 tablespoons olive oil and 1 tablespoon butter

1/2 cup pine nuts

2 to 3 shallots, chopped

1/2 cup chopped parsley

1 tablespoon chopped fresh mint, or 1 teaspoon dried

1 tablespoon chopped fresh dill, or 1 teaspoon dried

1/4 pound feta cheese, crumbled

1/4 pound kasseri cheese, grated

ROAST POTATOES

1 to 2 red potatoes per person, peeled and left whole

Salt and freshly ground black pepper, to taste

1 stick (4 ounces) unsalted butter

Lamb drippings

Preheat the oven to 350º. Remove the lamb from its marinade and dry with paper towels. Spread the stuffing on the inside of the lamb meat, covering nearly to the edges. Roll up the meat and tie with kitchen twine to maintain the shape. Place the lamb in a heatproof casserole or roasting pan; strain the marinade and pour over the lamb. Roast uncovered for about 2 to 2 1/2 hours. In Greek cooking, lamb is always eaten well-done-- never pink!!! The roast is done when it is fork tender or at an internal temperature of 160º. Remove the lamb from the pan and allow to rest at least 20 minutes before slicing. Raise the oven heat to 375º for the roast potatoes.

Heat the butter in a large, heavy skillet. Dry the potatoes well and cook in the butter until they are browned. Place the potatoes in the pan in which the lamb was cooked and bake them in the drippings for 30 to 40 minutes until they are tender.

To serve, slice the lamb and arrange on a heated platter. Place the potatoes around the outside. Pass the drippings separately. Greek drippings are rarely thickened but rather are usually served au jus.

Green beans are also good served this way.

2 pounds fresh asparagus, cleaned, tough bottoms removed

1/4 cup butter

1/2 cup Kasseri cheese, grated, or use parmesan

There is no lettuce in this salad of vegetables!

3 large, ripe tomatoes

1 large green or red pepper

2 cucumbers, peeled (and seeded if the seeds are large)

1 large red onion

1/2 cup olive oil

1/4 cup red wine vinegar

Fresh herbs, or dried (usually oregano and/or parsley)

1/4 pound feta cheese, crumbled

1/2 cup Kalamata olives, or any Greek olives

This Greek sweet bread is made twice a year. At Easter time it is decorated with red eggs; at New Year's it is called Vasilopeta and baked with a coin inside to bring good luck to the person in whose piece it is found. It is flavored with mahlep, made from the kernel of black cherries, and mastika, a Greek flavoring usually found where Greek deli items are sold. If these are unavailable, substitute cardamom for the mahlep and anise seed for the mastika.

SPARAGIA ME KASSERI
(Steamed Asparagus With Cream Cheese)

Cook the asparagus in boiling water until just tender. Drain well. Heat the butter in a small saucepan until it sizzles and begins to turn brown or burns. Pour the butter over the asparagus in a heated serving dish and top with the cheese. Serve immediately.

HORIATIKI SALATA
(Greek Vegetable Salad)

Cut the vegetables into small pieces, not into slices! Toss all the vegetables in a large bowl with the oil and vinegar. Add the herbs, cheese and olives. A little freshly ground black pepper might be nice, but taste before adding salt since the olives *and* the feta are salty! You could omit the feta if you like, since several items in this menu include cheese.

The "Greek way" is to dunk one's bread in the juices left behind on your plate!

TSOUREKIA
(Greek Sweet Bread)

Heat the oven to its lowest temperature and *turn it off.*

Bring the milk, sugar, butter and mahlep or cardamom to a boil. Cool to lukewarm.

Stir the yeast and 1 teaspoon sugar into the warm water and allow it to sit until foamy. Stir in the 1/4 cup of flour and allow to foam again. This mixture will rise a bit so use a 4-cup measure to contain the foam.

For 2 braided loaves or 1 ring loaf:

4 to 6 hardboiled eggs, dyed red (optional)

1 cup milk

1 cup sugar

1 stick (4 ounces) unsalted butter

1/8 teaspoon mahlep, crushed

1/2 cup warm water

1 teaspoon sugar

3 tablespoons active dry yeast

1/4 cup flour

2 eggs, beaten

Grated rind of 1 lemon

Dash of salt

1/8 teaspoon mastika, crushed

5 1/2 to 6 cups all purpose unbleached flour, approximately

1 egg plus 1 egg yolk for glaze before baking

Stir the 2 beaten eggs, lemon rind, salt and mastika into the lukewarm milk mixture, then add the yeast mixture and stir to blend.

If you are working with a food processor be sure that it has a capacity of 8 cups of flour or more, since this is a large amount of dough. Place 5 1/2 cups of the flour in the workbowl fitted with the dough blade. Have extra flour ready to add by tablespoons if the dough is too sticky. With the machine running slowly pour the liquid mixture through the feed tube until the dough gathers into a ball. Add extra flour as needed, only if the dough is too sticky to rotate. Allow the dough to rotate (knead) 30 to 40 seconds.

If you are working with a mixer place all the liquids in the bowl. Attach the pastry paddle and add half the flour while the machine is running, to form a batter. Now attach the dough hook and continue running the machine, adding flour a little at a time until the dough ball forms. Continue kneading for 3 to 4 minutes. The dough should clean the sides of the bowl and not be sticky.

Place the dough in a gallon-size plastic bag. Squeeze out all the air and place a wire twist at the *top* of the bag so that the dough can expand. Set the bag in the barely warm oven on a pot holder until the dough doubles in size--about 1 hour.

Open the bag, deflate the dough, reseal and allow to rise in the oven again until doubled, about 45 minutes.

Remove the dough from the bag, deflate it and form into two braided loaves or one large ring loaf. You may bake it in a large pan but the sides will brown better if you make a free-form loaf.

If you are using the red-dyed eggs insert them into the surface of the dough now so that they are about half concealed. Place the loaves on greased or parchment-lined baking sheets. Cover with oiled plastic wrap and allow to double in size again.

Preheat the oven to 350°. Beat the egg and extra yolk well and gently brush the entire surface of the loaf. Sprinkle with sesame seeds or slivered almonds for decoration, if you like. Bake for 30 to 40 minutes until the crust is dark and shiny (from the egg glaze). An instant read thermometer should register at least 180° in the center of the loaf. Cool on a rack.

2 sticks (8 ounces) unsalted butter, at room temperature

1 cup vegetable oil

1 cup granulated sugar

3/4 cup orange juice

1 teaspoon grated orange rind

1 egg, well beaten

1 teaspoon baking soda

5 1/2 to 6 cups all purpose flour

1 cup ground nuts

1/2 teaspoon ground cinnamon

1/4 teaspoon ground nutmeg, freshly grated, if possible

DIPPING SYRUP

2 cups honey

1/2 cup water

1/2 cinnamon stick

A few whole cloves

A thumb-size piece of orange peel

PHOENIKA YEMISTA
(Greek Stuffed Honey Cookies)

Place the butter and the oil in the bowl of an electric mixer fitted with the pastry paddle or the beaters. Beat for 20 minutes! Add the sugar and beat for another 10 minutes. Add the juice, rind and egg, and beat just to blend well.

Remove the bowl from the mixer. Stir the baking soda into one cup of the flour. Using a wooden spoon or rubber spatula stir that flour into the batter and continue to add flour and stir until the dough is the consistency of a molded cookie dough--that is, it is neither sticky nor falling apart. Test it by rolling a small amount between your palms. It is hard to give an exact measurement of flour; I often bake one or two on a cookie sheet to test the "holding power" of the shape. You might need more flour than called for depending on the humidity, brand of flour and so on.

Preheat oven to 350º.

Stir together the ground nuts, cinnamon and nutmeg. Shape golf ball-size pieces of dough into ovals. Press your finger into the center to make an indentation and add 1/2 teaspoon of the nut filling. Press the dough to close the hole over the filling. Place the ovals on unbuttered cookie sheets about 2 inches apart and bake for about 20 minutes until golden brown. Cool on racks to room temperature.

Make the dipping syrup by heating the honey, water, cinnamon stick, cloves, and orange peel over medium heat for 15 minutes. Strain the syrup and use for dipping while it is warm. You may keep it in a closed jar in the refrigerator.

Dip the cookies in warm syrup and drain on cooling racks set over cookie sheets or wax paper, etc., to protect your countertop. The cookies may be served after draining briefly. You may store the cookies in an airtight container or freeze them but *do not dip them if they are to be stored*--they should be dipped at the time of serving!

4 sticks (1 pound) unsalted butter, at room temperature

1/3 cup superfine sugar, or powdered sugar

2 tablespoons brandy

3/4 cup blanched, toasted almonds, finely chopped

3 1/2 to 4 cups cake flour or pastry flour

60 whole cloves

2 pounds powdered sugar

KOURAMBIEDES
(Greek Butter Cookies)

In the bowl of an electric mixer fitted with the pastry paddle or beaters beat the butter for 30 minutes! It should turn white and fluffy and make a "slapping" sound against the sides of the bowl as it mixes. Gradually add the superfine sugar and beat for 20 more minutes. Add the brandy and beat until well-blended. Remove the bowl from the mixer.

Using a wooden spoon or a rubber spatula stir in the chopped almonds. Stir the flour into the mixture until it resembles a molded cookie dough--that is, it should be neither sticky nor falling apart. Test by rolling a small amount between your palms. Add a little more flour if necessary. It is not a bad idea to test bake one or two cookies to see how they hold their shape.

Preheat the oven to 350º.

Form pieces of dough about the size of a large walnut or just slightly larger into crescent shapes. Place a whole clove in the center of each crescent. Place on an ungreased cookie sheet and bake for about 15 minutes or until the cookies just begin to turn golden, but do not let them brown on top.

While the cookies are baking sift some of the powdered sugar onto a wax paper-covered table or large cutting board. Carefully remove the cookies from the baking sheet and place onto the powdered sugar. Allow the cookies to sit in the sugar for 5 minutes and sprinkle more powdered sugar *generously* over the top of the cookies. They should be well-coated in the sugar. Allow them to cool completely while still in the sugar!

Traditionally, these are served in paper muffin cups. They freeze well but will need to be resugared before serving.

Pizzarollas
Border Pizza
Mushroom, Sweet Red Pepper and Sausage Deep Dish Pizza
K.T.'s Pizza Jeannette
Ginger Ice Cream
Aunt Ethel's Chocolate Macaroons

APRIL FOOL'S DAY PIZZA PARTY

indful of the constant craze for pizza we decided to put together an almost all pizza menu! What better day to reveal your secret menu as your guests arrive? Of course, you can enjoy it at any time of year, even going so far as to assign a pizza to be brought by each of several (presumably good) friends.

The pizzas reflect a wide range of nationalities. Begin with two appetizer "pizzas"--one from Provence, France, laden with onions and olives and the other a quasi Greek-Italian combination called Pizzarollas with pizza flavors on the inside but phyllo on the outside! Sneak in a "Border Pizza," a combination of a masa dough crust, refried bean topping and a rich, homemade enchilada sauce. For the "main course" turn to the heartland of America, Chicago, where deep-dish pizza was born! All this is gutsy, satisfying fare that could be accompanied with a hearty salad and lots of good wine or beer.

We finish this menu with a refreshing and light dessert--Ginger Ice Cream. And, knowing that there are the hardcore few who cannot resist that chocolate urge, we offer the recipe for a batch of homemade Chocolate Macaroons!

Diane f Morgan

1 pound phyllo sheets

1 pound Italian sausage--hot, mild or a combination

Optional: 1/2 pound pepperoni in place of the Italian sausage

1/4 pound mozzarella cheese, grated

1/2 pound fresh mushrooms or 1 4-ounce can button mushrooms, sliced thinly

1 2-1/4-ounce can sliced black olives

1 8-ounce can tomato sauce

2 teaspoons dried oregano

2 teaspoons dried basil

2 teaspoons olive oil

1/2 pound unsalted butter, melted

PIZZAROLLAS

Thaw phyllo overnight in the refrigerator.

Remove sausage from its casing, if any, and cook over medium heat to render out the fat. Crumble the meat as you cook it. Place the meat in a colander to drain. (If you are using pepperoni just chop it coarsely by hand or in a food processor--no cooking is necessary.)

If you are using fresh mushrooms cook them without fat in a large saute pan over medium heat until they give up their moisture; when all the liquid evaporates remove from the heat.

Drain canned mushrooms, if using, and the olives.

Mix together all ingredients except the phyllo and butter. Taste and adjust seasonings to your liking, adding more dried herbs if you like. The mixture should be thick, not watery.

Cut the sheets of phyllo into 4 equal pieces across the shorter side of the dough. To assemble the pizzarollas, butter a strip of the dough, place another strip on top of that one and butter it, too. Place a tablespoon of the filling at one end of the dough and roll 2 or 3 turns to cover the filling. Now fold the sides of the strips in about 1/2 an inch and continue rolling to the end of the dough. Place on an ungreased cookie sheet, lightly butter the tops of the rolls and bake at 375º until golden brown--about 20 minutes. Serve hot or at least warm.

These may be frozen and baked later if you like. Freeze them unbaked. I use a plastic 9x13 inch container with a lid and place the rolls in layers between sheets of waxed paper. Bake frozen at the same temperature; they will take an extra 5 to 10 minutes to bake.

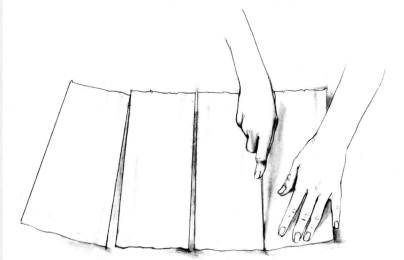

DOUGH

3/4 cup warm water

1 tablespoon active dry yeast

1 cup all purpose unbleached flour

1 cup masa harina (a prepared corn flour sold in many supermarkets)

1 teaspoon kosher salt

2 tablespoons lard or olive oil

SAUCE

3 tablespoons lard or bacon fat

1 small onion, coarsely chopped

2 cloves garlic, minced

3 cups water or meat stock

1 teaspoon ground cumin

1 teaspoon dried leaf oregano

1 teaspoon salt (omit if using canned broth)

1 teaspoon sugar

1 6-ounce bag dried mild chilies (such as New Mexico, California or Pasilla varieties frequently sold under the "Don Pancho" label--names vary considerably, so experiment)

TOPPING

1/2 regular size (16-ounce) can refried beans (or make your own)

3 scallions, thinly sliced

1 ripe avocado, peeled and sliced

A few thinly sliced jalapeño rings (optional)

1 cup freshly grated hard cheese, such as parmesan or dry jack

2 to 3 cups grated medium cheddar or monterey jack cheese

BORDER PIZZA

Here is a "pizza" inspired by my love of some of the most basic Mexican staples--corn, beans and chilies. I think that it tastes terrific, partly because of the homemade chili sauce. As always, though, feel free to use a canned enchilada sauce if time is too short or your grocer cannot provide you with the mild dried chilies.

The sauce may be made days ahead of time if you like. Rinse the chilies, place them on a cookie sheet and warm in a 300º oven for 5 or 6 minutes to soften them. Remove from the oven, cut off the stems and cut across each chili in 2 or 3 places so that the seeds may be shaken out.

In a 2 quart or larger saucepan heat the cooking fat. Cook the onion and garlic until wilted. Add the water or stock, cumin, oregano, salt if using, sugar and chilies. Cover and cook for 30 minutes.

Purée the sauce in a blender or food processor, then force the sauce through a sieve to extract the seeds and bits of skin which remain. Taste for salt and sugar (it should not be sweet--the sugar is used only to prevent bitterness from the chili skin). Refrigerate. Keeps for at least two weeks.

To make the dough, stir the yeast into the warm water to dissolve.

If you are using a food processor proceed to place all the dry ingredients in the workbowl fitted with the metal blade. Have a little extra flour ready in case your dough is too sticky and cannot rotate inside the workbowl. Add the olive oil to the yeast mixture, stir, and as the machine is running, slowly pour the liquids through the feed tube as quickly as the flour absorbs them. If you hear "sloshing" you are pouring too quickly. When the dough ball forms and begins regular rotation allow the machine to run for 45 to 60 seconds.

If you are using a mixer, place the liquids in the bowl and fit the machine with the pastry paddle (if available) to speed the dough formation. Add about half the total dry ingredients and run on low speed to obtain a batter-like consistency. Now remove the paddle, fit the dough hook and continue adding flour until a dough ball forms. Continue kneading for about 6 to 8 minutes. The dough should clean the sides of the bowl.

Place the dough in a gallon-size plastic bag, squeeze out all the air and place a wire twist at the *top* of the bag so that the dough has room to expand. Allow the dough to rise until it has doubled in size--probably from 45 minutes to 1 hour 30 minutes.

Remove the dough from the bag, deflate thoroughly ("punch down") and press (or roll out to fit) the dough into a greased or cornmeal coated 12- to 14-inch pan (we have used a 12-inch skillet with sloped sides quite successfully). Heat the refried beans just enough to soften them. Spread over the dough. Top with about 1 1/2 cups of the chili sauce (if the sauce seems too thin, thicken it by mixing equal parts of cornstarch and water; bring the sauce to a boil and stir in a little of the dissolved cornstarch, repeating if necessary), reserving the remaining sauce for another use. Finish by arranging the scallions, avocados, jalapeño rings, if using, and the cheeses. Allow to rest while preheating oven to 450º.

Bake the pizza in a 450º oven until the dough is well-browned around the edges. Allow to rest 5 minutes before serving.

Here is my favorite tomato sauce recipe for pizza or pasta. I make it in large quantities and freeze it for convenient use later. If you are short on time by all means use your favorite prepared sauce or the Quick Tomato Sauce which appears in the Pizza Jeannette in this menu.

For 1 14-inch pizza:

SAUCE (makes about 1 quart)

3 tablespoons olive oil

1 large onion, peeled and diced

1 rib celery, peeled and diced

1 carrot, peeled and diced

4 tablespoons freshly minced parsley

3 large cloves garlic, peeled and minced

1 bay leaf

2 tablespoons chopped fresh basil or 2 teaspoons dried

1 1/2 teaspoons dried oregano

1 teaspoon dried thyme

3 28-ounce cans whole plum tomatoes, drained and chopped

1 6-ounce can tomato paste

Salt, freshly ground black pepper and sugar, to taste

Cornstarch for thickening, if needed

MUSHROOM, SWEET RED PEPPER AND SAUSAGE DEEP DISH PIZZA

In a large saucepan heat the olive oil. Add all the ingredients except the tomatoes, tomato paste, salt, pepper and sugar. Cook, stirring occasionally, over moderate heat, partially covered until soft but not browned--about 20 to 30 minutes.

Add the tomatoes, tomato paste and seasonings and simmer, covered, for 1 hour 30 minutes to 2 hours. Stir every 15 minutes to prevent scorching. Taste and adjust seasonings.

If the sauce seems too thin blend 2 or 3 tablespoons of cornstarch with an equal amount of water. Stir a little into the sauce as it simmers, using only the amount of thickener needed. When the sauce is cool, purée it by passing it through a food mill or using a food processor fitted with the metal chopping blade.

One hour 30 minutes to 2 hours before serving time make the pizza dough. Stir the yeast into the warm (*not* hot) water and let stand for 5 minutes.

If you are using a food processor to make the dough proceed to place all the dry ingredients in the workbowl. Have a little extra flour ready in case your dough is too sticky and cannot rotate in the workbowl. Add the oil to the water-yeast mixture and stir. With the machine running slowly pour the liquids through the feed tube as quickly as the flour absorbs it. If you hear "sloshing" you are pouring too quickly. When the dough ball forms and begins regular rotation inside the workbowl allow the machine to run for 45 to 60 seconds.

If you are using a mixer, place the liquids in the bowl and fit the machine with the pastry paddle (if available) to speed the dough formation. Add about half the total flour and run on low speed to obtain a batter-like consistency. Now remove the paddle, fit the dough hook and continue adding flour until a dough ball forms. Continue kneading for about 6 to 8 minutes. The dough should clean the sides of the bowl.

Place the dough in a gallon-size plastic bag, squeeze out all the air and place a wire twist at the *top* of the bag so that the dough has room to expand. Allow the dough to rise until it has doubled in size--probably from 45 minutes to 1 hour 30 minutes.

Remove the dough from the bag, deflate thoroughly ("punch down") and press the dough onto the bottom and up the sides of an oiled 14-inch round deep dish pizza pan. Allow to rise again for 15 to 20 minutes while you prepare the toppings for the pizza.

DOUGH

1 cup warm water

1 tablespoon active dry yeast

1/4 cup olive oil

2 cups all purpose unbleached flour

1 cup semolina flour (available in some supermarkets and many health-food or nutrition centers)

1/2 cup yellow corn meal

1 teaspoon salt

TOPPINGS

6 tablespoons olive oil, divided

1 pound bulk Italian sausage

2 sweet red peppers, cut into thin strips

1 medium onion, thinly sliced

3/4 pound fresh mushrooms, thinly sliced

Pinch of cayenne pepper

2 tablespoons dry vermouth

1 teaspoon flour

Salt and pepper if desired

1 pound mozzarella cheese, grated

1/2 cup grated parmesan cheese

Preheat the oven to 500°. In a large sauté pan heat 2 tablespoons of the olive oil and cook the sausage until it is no longer pink, breaking up any large pieces. Using a slotted spoon remove the meat from the pan, leaving the fat in the pan. Add the sweet red peppers and the onion and sauté until they are softened. Turn the contents of the pan into a colander to drain.

Add 2 more tablespoons of olive oil to the pan and sauté the mushrooms until they give up their liquid. Add the cayenne and the vermouth and cook until the juices evaporate. Sprinkle on the flour, salt and pepper, stir to combine and transfer to the colander.

To assemble the pizza gently brush the surface of the dough with 2 tablespoons of olive oil. Sprinkle on half the cheeses. Add the sausage, then the vegetables. Pour on about 3 cups of the sauce and top with the remaining cheese.

Bake until golden brown--probably 15 to 18 minutes. Let stand 5 minutes before serving to firm slightly.

DM

CRUST

1 3/4 cups all purpose unbleached flour

1 teaspoon kosher salt

1 stick (4 ounces) unsalted butter

1/2 cup cold water

1 whole egg

1 teaspoon anchovy paste

1 teaspoon dijon mustard

FILLING

1/4 cup olive oil

2 pounds onions, peeled and sliced

1 teaspoon kosher salt

2 to 3 tablespoons freshly grated parmesan cheese

2/3 cup quick tomato sauce (recipe follows)

3 ounces Roquefort or blue cheese

24 green or black olives, sliced

SAUCE

5 1/2 tablespoons olive oil

1 tablespoon minced shallot or onion

1/2 cup tomato paste

1 1/3 cups chicken broth or water

1 bay leaf

2 teaspoons herbes de Provence

Salt and pepper, to taste

Freshly ground nutmeg, to taste

K.T.'S PIZZA JEANNETTE

This is my adaptation of a Provencale pizza of Simone Beck. The crust for it is a pâté brisée, or tart pastry, topped by a healthy amount of slow-cooked, sweet onions, a bit of tomato sauce and cheeses. It is one of my favorite, most comforting foods!

Divide the butter into eight pieces and freeze for 15 minutes. Place the flour and salt in the workbowl of a food processor fitted with the metal blade. Add the butter and pulse the machine until the pieces of butter average between a lima bean and a pea in size. With the machine running pour in the cold water--taking about 5 to 10 seconds to do that--and stop the machine before the pastry forms a ball!

Roll out the dough on a floured work surface. There will be enough dough to make 1 10x16-inch rectangle (for a cookie sheet) or 2 smaller round crusts; 9-inch round tart pans with removable bottoms work nicely. Place the dough into the pan(s) and trim the edges. Prick the bottom well with a fork. Preheat the oven to 400º. Place the prepared crust in the freezer for 15 minutes. Freezing pastry doughs helps to prevent shrinking during baking.

Remove the crust from the freezer and cover it with aluminum foil. Place pie weights or rice or dried beans on the foil and bake the crust for 10 minutes. Remove the weights and foil and bake another 10 minutes. Beat the egg and anchovy paste together, brush it over the crust and bake for another 2 to 3 minutes. Remove the crust from the oven and set aside.

About an hour and a quarter before you want to serve, heat the olive oil in a large sauté pan or skillet. Add the onions, tossing to coat. Cover and cook over low heat for 15 minutes, stirring occasionally. Uncover the pan and cook over moderate heat 30 more minutes, stirring occasionally. Stir in the salt and remove from the heat.

To make the sauce heat the olive oil in a medium saucepan, add the onions or shallots and cook until wilted. Stir in all other ingredients and simmer uncovered for 15 to 20 minutes. If the sauce seems too thin, then simmer uncovered until desired consistency is achieved. Remove the bay leaf. The sauce may be stored for several days in the refrigerator or months in the freezer.

Preheat the oven to 350º. Sprinkle the parmesan cheese over the bottom of the crust, topped by half the onions. Spread all the sauce over the onions, then cover with the remaining onions, Roquefort and olives.

Bake until the cheese is melted and the onions are warm, about 20 minutes. Let rest several minutes before serving.

K. T.

GINGER ICE CREAM

1 cup milk

1 cup cream

1/3 cup sugar

1 tablespoon flour

1/4 teaspoon salt

1/2 teaspoon ground ginger

2 egg yolks

3/4 teaspoon vanilla extract

1/4 cup preserved ginger in syrup, finely chopped, including a little syrup

1 cup heavy cream, softly whipped

1/2 teaspoon freshly squeezed lemon juice

Scald the milk and cream in a heavy-bottomed saucepan. Remove from the heat and whisk in the dry ingredients. Lightly beat the egg yolks in a heat-proof glass or stainless steel bowl or in the top of a non-aluminum double boiler. Gradually add the hot milk mixture, whisking to combine. Place over simmering water and cook, stirring often, until the mixture has slightly thickened and coats a spoon. This may take up to 20 minutes. Remove from the heat.

Cool, stirring occasionally. Add the vanilla and preserved ginger when cool. Gently fold in the whipped cream and lemon juice.

Freeze according to the directions for your ice cream freezer. Makes 1 quart.

NOTE: Preserved ginger in syrup may be purchased in many Oriental groceries.

AUNT ETHEL'S CHOCOLATE MACAROONS

My aunt always kept a jar of these cookies in her kitchen. They are one of my fondest memories from childhood. Keep them stored airtight or they will dry out quickly.

2 large egg whites, at room temperature

1/4 teaspoon salt

3/4 cup granulated sugar

1/2 teaspoon vanilla extract

1 1/2 ounces unsweetened chocolate, melted

1 1/2 cups finely shredded coconut

Preheat oven to 325º.

Using a mixer, beat the egg whites and salt until foamy. Gradually add the sugar, two tablespoons at a time, beating well after each addition. Continue beating until the mixture holds stiff peaks, probably 5 to 10 minutes. Add the vanilla, then the melted chocolate.

Remove the bowl from the mixer stand and fold in the coconut using a rubber spatula.

Drop from a teaspoon onto a parchment paper liner on a cookie sheet (or use non-stick baking sheets). Bake 20 minutes. Cool for 5 minutes on the paper; then transfer to a rack to complete the cooling. Makes about 3 dozen cookies.

East-West Black Mushroom Soup
Artichoke and Ricotta Cheese Pie
Asparagus Salad with Pine Nuts
Chocolate-Ginger Angel Food Cake

———————————————◆———————————————

SPRING LUNCHEON

*L*uncheons seem to have been left behind by the furious pace at which we run these days! If you have or can make the time, a leisurely midday meal has a great deal of charm. We have designed a spring luncheon menu that would work equally well as a buffet or as a sit-down affair. We urge you to vary it according to your whims and schedule!

The first course is a French-style soup with Chinese mushrooms! It is a very successful marriage of French technique and Oriental ingredients. Small portions are advised as the soup is rich.

Your efforts will be justly rewarded in making the Artichoke and Ricotta Cheese Pie. In this dish, golden, flaky phyllo pastry encloses a creamy blend of cheese and tender artichoke hearts, delicately flavored with scallions and tarragon. Keep this one in mind when you are planning a brunch or light supper menu, too!

I always equate fresh asparagus with spring. Diane's Asparagus Salad with Pine Nuts is a perfect way to enjoy the first of the season. Its delicate dressing permits the flavor of the asparagus to really shine.

As if all this were not enough, Kathleen has created a sensational Chocolate Ginger Angel Food Cake, served atop a purée of fresh rhubarb! It is a sublime combination of flavors, as light and fresh as spring.

Do not forget to occasionally take time out to enjoy something which is gradually disappearing from our lives--a leisurely luncheon.

Audrey Ursomanon

6 cups chicken stock, preferably homemade

1 teaspoon kosher salt

Freshly ground black pepper, to taste

12 fresh mushrooms, cleaned and left whole

12 dried Chinese black mushrooms, whole

2 ribs celery, cut into 1 inch lengths

1 carrot, peeled, cut into 1 inch lengths

1 medium onion, peeled, left whole, stuck with 2 cloves

2 cups heavy cream

1/4 cup Port wine

1 1/2 teaspoons unsalted butter, at room temperature

1 1/2 teaspoons flour

2 egg yolks

1/2 cup heavy cream

1 tablespoon freshly minced parsley, as garnish

EAST-WEST BLACK MUSHROOM SOUP

This recipe was the creation of my friend and mentor, Alma Lach, and has always been a favorite of mine!

Combine the stock, seasonings, fresh and dried mushrooms, celery, carrot and onion in a 6 quart pot. Bring to a boil and simmer partially covered for 30 minutes.

In the meantime, combine the 2 cups of heavy cream and the Port in a large saucepan and bring to a boil. Boil until the mixture is reduced by half; do not allow the cream to boil over the pan! Reserve off the heat.

Strain the broth through a fine mesh sieve. Remove the black mushrooms and slice them thinly. Discard the other vegetables.

Knead together the butter and flour. Put the strained broth and the sliced mushrooms back into the pot, add the cream-port mixture and bring to a simmer. Add the butter-flour mixture to the pot, stirring until it dissolves completely and thickens the soup. The soup can be made ahead to this point and refrigerated.

When ready to serve heat the soup without boiling. Combine the egg yolks and the 1/2 cup cream and mix thoroughly. Stir a ladle of the hot soup into this yolk-cream mixture to temper it, then pour all back into the soup. Stir to blend. Taste and adjust seasonings. Pour into a tureen or ladle into individual soup bowls, garnish and serve. Makes 6-8 servings.

DM

ARTICHOKE AND RICOTTA CHEESE PIE

2 9-ounce packages frozen artichoke hearts

1/2 cup water

Pinch salt

1/4 cup minced green onion

1 tablespoon olive oil

1 pound whole-milk ricotta cheese

1 cup grated Gruyère cheese

3/4 cup grated parmesan cheese

1/2 cup sour cream

4 large eggs

1/2 teaspoon dried tarragon

Salt and freshly ground white pepper, to taste

2 cups olive oil

1 pound phyllo pastry, thawed overnight in the refrigerator

Bring the water and salt to a boil in a large saucepan. Add the frozen artichoke hearts and cook, covered, for 5 minutes. Drain and reserve.

Sauté the green onions in 1 tablespoon of olive oil briefly. In a large bowl combine all three cheeses, sour cream, eggs, tarragon and the sautéed onions. Halve or quarter the drained artichoke hearts, depending on their size. Add them and the salt and pepper to the cheese mixture.

Brush a 10-inch springform pan generously with olive oil. Place 4 sheets of phyllo on top of each other, brushing each first with olive oil. Place them in the pan with the edges overhanging. Repeat with another 4 sheets of phyllo and place them at a right angle to the first set so that their edges hang over the other two sides of the pan.

Add half the cheese mixture to the pan. Top with 8 more sheets of phyllo in the same manner as before. Add the remaining cheese miixture and fold the phyllo edges in toward the center of the pan to hold in the filling.

Oil the remaining phyllo sheets and place them on top of the pie, arranging them as before. Tuck their edges in all the way around; it may be easier to release the springform side to accomplish this. Relock the springform when you have tucked in all the edges.

Preheat the oven to 400°. Place the pie on a cookie sheet or jelly roll pan so any leaking oil does not burn on the bottom of the oven. Brush the top of the pie with olive oil and bake in the center of the oven for about 40 minutes, or until an instant read thermometer registers 160°. Allow the pie to rest out of the oven for at least 10 to 15 minutes before removing the springform side. The pie is good served warm or at room temperature. You may reheat it, but the phyllo will not be as crisp the second time around. Serves 8 to 10.

To serve 6 to 8 persons:

2 pounds fresh asparagus

1/4 cup pine nuts

1/2 cup olive oil

2 tablespoons freshly squeezed lemon juice

1 large clove garlic, minced

1 teaspoon kosher salt

1/2 teaspoon sugar

Freshly ground black pepper, to taste

1 tablespoon minced fresh oregano
or 1 teaspoon dried

1 tablespoon minced fresh basil
or 1 teaspoon dried

ASPARAGUS SALAD WITH PINE NUTS

Cut tough ends from the asparagus and peel the stalks (using a vegetable or asparagus peeler) from just below the tip to the base. Bring a large pan of salted water to a boil, add the asparagus and cook for 2 to 4 minutes until the asparagus is just tender. *Immediately* remove from the boiling water and plunge into a bowl of ice water. After one minute drain and dry on paper towels, then cut into 2 inch lengths and reserve.

In a dry, heavy-bottomed skillet toast the pine nuts until evenly brown, shaking the pan often to toss the nuts. Set aside on a plate to cool to room temperature.

Combine the vinaigrette ingredients in a jar with a tight-fitting lid. Shake well, *taste*, and adjust seasonings. Reserve at room temperature.

About 20 minutes before serving toss the asparagus with the well-shaken vinaigrette and sprinkle the pine nuts on top. Toss again just before serving.

DM

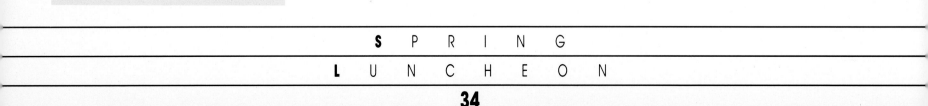

The base of this cake is Maida Heatter's beautiful Chocolate Angel Food Cake, but I have had a few ideas and taken a few liberties!

1 cup less 2 tablespoons sifted cake flour

1 1/2 cups sifted powdered sugar

1/2 cup unsweetened cocoa powder

1 tablespoon dry powdered instant espresso

1 1/2 cups egg whites (about 10 to 12 eggs), at room temperature

1/2 teaspoon salt

1 1/2 teaspoons cream of tartar

1 cup sugar

1/2 ounce (about a walnut size piece) unpeeled fresh ginger, chopped finely

3 ounces crystallized ginger, chopped finely

RHUBARB SAUCE

6 cups chopped fresh rhubarb

1/2 cup sugar

2/3 cup water

2/3 cup Triple Sec

Few drops red food coloring

Lightly whipped cream or crème fraiche, if desired

CHOCOLATE-GINGER ANGEL FOOD CAKE

Preheat the oven to 375º. Use a 10-inch angel food cake pan with a removable bottom, at least 4 inches deep. Do *not* butter the pan.

Sift together three times the flour, powdered sugar, cocoa and instant espresso. Reserve.

Beat the egg whites with the salt and cream of tartar until they hold a firm shape but are not dry. Transfer them to a large, wide bowl.

Stir together the sifted dry ingredients and the sugar. Sift them gradually over the egg whites as you gently fold the mixture together using a large rubber spatula. Sprinkle in the two chopped gingers toward the end of the folding process. Fold only as much as is necessary to prevent deflating the egg whites.

Pour the mixture into the ungreased pan. Using a table knife, or long narrow spatula, cut through the batter in wide circles around the pan to remove large air bubbles.

Bake in a preheated 375º oven for 40 minutes or until the cake just springs back when poked with a finger. An instant read thermometer will probably register 180º or more. Remove the cake from the oven and suspend it upside down over the neck of a bottle until thoroughly cool.

To remove the cake from the pan run a long-bladed knife around the sides to loosen it. Pull the cake out of the pan and run the knife around the bottom to loosen.

To make the sauce place the rhubarb pieces, sugar, water and Triple Sec in a large, non-aluminum saucepan. Bring to a boil, reduce to a simmer and cook, uncovered, for 30 minutes. Purée in a food processor or blender. The sauce should seem slightly thickened since it will be on the plate along with whipped cream or crème fraiche. If it seems too thin cook it down a bit. Stir in a little food coloring if you like, then cool the sauce.

To serve, cover each dessert plate with some rhubarb sauce, then top with a little lightly whipped cream or crème fraiche drizzled down the center of the plate. Top with a slice of the angel food cake. Makes about 12 servings.

K. T.

Feta "Cookies"
Chicken Terrine with Pistachios and Curried Mayonnaise
Miniature Grilled Cheese Sandwiches
Semolina-Sour Cream Bread
Cheddar, Bacon and Cashew Butter Sandwiches
Whole Wheat Starter Sandwich Loaf
Assorted Tea Sandwiches
Chocolate Pecan Ring Loaf

———————————————◆———————————————

A TEA

O ne of the most surprising food trends in recent years has been the introduction of Afternoon Tea in some fine hotels and restaurants across America. It surprises me because the ritual of Afternoon Tea is in such striking contrast to the style of eating-on-the-run made famous by fast food outlets. We have designed a menu to take advantage of several of our favorite foods--foods beautiful and flavorful enough to become part of a charming ritual-- Afternoon Tea!

We have provided you with a plethora of ideas and recipes to work with. Select just a few, or get involved and make all the recipes for an elaborate, glorious presentation. The majority of the foods can be made ahead: only a few last minute details require your attention. Georgia's Feta "Cookies" can be frozen unbaked; Dan's Chocolate Pecan Ring Loaf freezes well after baking; you can make my Chicken Terrine up to five days before serving so it needs only slicing on the day of the tea! The Semolina-Sour Cream Bread and Whole Wheat Starter Bread both freeze well or can be made up to two days in advance without freezing. If you are short on time, buy good quality breads to use with the Miniature Grilled Cheese Sandwiches, and Cheddar, Bacon and Cashew Butter Sandwiches. However, Dan's breads are some of the best I know so do not pass those recipes by. My Curried Mayonnaise (to accompany the Chicken Terrine) and the Cashew Butter for Kathleen's sandwich may be prepared several days in advance. On the day of the party you need only sauté the onions for the Miniature Grilled Cheese Sandwiches, put together Audrey's assortment of easy Tea Sandwiches, bake the Feta "Cookies" and slice the Chicken Terrine. The assorted Tea Sandwiches can be assembled and held fresh for two hours under a lightly-dampened paper towel covered with plastic wrap.

By planning ahead you can relax and enjoy your guests and some very good food. Brew several choices of good teas if you like, and serve in elegant china teapots.

Diane J. Morgan

For 12 miniature sandwiches:

1/2 cup raisins

1/3 cup Port wine

2 large onions, thinly sliced

2 tablespoons vegetable oil

3 ounces crumbled blue cheese--such as Maytag, Oregon Blue or another good quality cheese

Semolina-Sour Cream Bread (recipe follows) or another firm-textured bread

Softened butter

MINIATURE GRILLED CHEESE SANDWICHES

These little sandwiches fall into my category of "comforting foods." I get a happy feeling just thinking about eating them! I love grilled cheese sandwiches for a simple supper and thought that they would make a charming addition to our tea. The filling is unusual, and, thanks to Dan, the breads are great (try the Semolina-Sour Cream Bread for breakfast toast!). The sandwiches are easy to prepare once the bread is done, and they can even be frozen. These reheat quite well.

Soak the raisins in the Port wine for several hours or overnight. Drain before using.

Sauté the onions slowly in the vegetable oil until they just begin to brown. Set aside.

Assemble the sandwiches by dividing the cheese, raisins and onions evenly among three slices of bread. Top with three more slices of bread. Butter the top of the sandwiches with softened butter and place buttered side down on a hot griddle. Butter the other side. Grill sandwiches until nicely browned on both sides. Divide each sandwich into quarters and serve immediately.

K.T.

For 16 miniature sandwiches:

4 ounces sharp cheddar cheese (such as Tillamook aged, Vermont or Black Diamond)

12 slices pepper bacon, cooked until crisp, then drained

1 cup toasted, unsalted cashew nuts

8 slices Starter Whole Wheat bread (recipe follows) or another firm whole wheat bread

Softened butter

CHEDDAR, BACON AND CASHEW BUTTER SANDWICHES

Slice the cheese thinly.

In the workbowl of a food processor fitted with the metal blade process the nuts until they form a butter, probably 2 to 3 minutes. Add a few drops of vegetable oil to thin the butter slightly if necessary.

Spread four slices of the bread with cashew butter, reserving any extra for your morning toast! Add the sliced cheese and bacon. Top with the remaining bread slices. Butter the tops with softened butter. Place buttered sides down on a preheated griddle. Butter the other sides. Grill until browned on both sides.

Divide into quarters and serve immediately.

K.T.

For 1 large pullman loaf or 2 5x9 inch loaves:

1 cup (8 ounces) sour cream

1 cup milk

2 teaspoons sugar

1 tablespoon active dry yeast

2 cups semolina flour (available in some supermarkets and usually in health-food stores or nutrition centers)

3 cups all purpose unbleached flour, approximately

2 teaspoons kosher salt

1/2 teaspoon baking soda

SEMOLINA-SOUR CREAM BREAD

Warm the sour cream, milk and sugar in a saucepan or microwave until an instant read thermometer registers 105° to 115°. Stir in the yeast and allow to stand until foamy, 5 to 10 minutes.

If you are working with a food processor place the remaining ingredients in the workbowl fitted with the dough blade, if so equipped. Stir up the yeast mixture and, with the machine running, slowly pour it into the dry ingredients. If you hear "sloshing" you are pouring too quickly. Allow the dough ball to form and when it begins regular rotation around the inside of the machine allow it to "knead" like this for 45 to 60 seconds, adding a little flour if necessary to control stickiness.

If you are working with a mixer, place the liquids in the bowl. With the machine fitted with the pastry paddle, add 1/2 the dry ingredients and run on low speed until a batter has formed. Switch to the dough hook and continue adding flour until a dough ball forms. Continue kneading for 6 to 8 minutes. The dough should clean the sides of the bowl.

Place the dough in a gallon-size plastic bag, squeeze all the air out of the bag, and attach a wire twist at the *top* of the bag so that the dough has room to expand. Allow to double in size, probably about 45 minutes to 1 1/2 hours.

Remove the dough from the bag and deflate thoroughly ("punch down"). Shape into one large or two smaller loaves and place in greased bread pan(s). (A "pullman" pan makes a nice shape which has a perfectly square cross section; it comes with a lid which is put in place when the dough has risen almost to the top of the pan. A short continued rise is given, then the loaf is baked. The lid ensures a flat top, hence a square slice!) Cover the loaves with oiled or sprayed plastic wrap and allow the dough to rise until it is just above the top of the pan if you are using a regular style bread pan.

While the loaves are rising preheat the oven to 375°. When ready to bake you may, if you like, gently brush beaten whole egg over the top of the loaves for a brown and shiny look, unless you are using a pullman pan with a lid. Bake until golden on top, about 40 minutes for two smaller loaves or 50 to 60 minutes for one large pullman loaf. An instant read thermometer should read at least 180° when inserted into the center of the loaf. Remove from the pan, and cool on a rack.

For 1 large pullman loaf or 2 5x9 inch loaves:

2 cups warm water

2 cups whole wheat flour

1 teaspoon active dry yeast

2 tablespoons vegetable oil

2 1/3 cups bread flour, approximately

1 cup whole wheat flour

2 1/2 teaspoons kosher salt

WHOLE WHEAT STARTER SANDWICH LOAF

To make the starter stir together the first three ingredients in a mixing bowl. Cover with plastic wrap and let stand at room temperature for about 24 hours.

Add the vegetable oil to the starter mixture and stir it down.

If you are working with a food processor place the remaining flours and the salt in the workbowl fitted with the dough blade, if so equipped. With the machine running slowly pour the starter into the workbowl. When the dough forms a ball and begins to rotate regularly inside the workbowl, allow it to continue kneading in this manner for 45 to 60 seconds, adding flour as necessary if the dough is too sticky to rotate.

If you are using a mixer, place the starter mixture in the bowl. Fit the machine with the dough hook. With the machine running, add the salt, the whole wheat flour and bread flour until a dough ball forms. Allow to continue kneading for 6 to 8 minutes. The dough should clean the sides of the bowl.

Place the dough in a gallon-size plastic bag, squeeze all the air out of the bag and place a wire twist at the *top* of the bag so that the dough has room to expand. Allow to rise until double its original size, probably 45 minutes to 1 1/2 hours.

Remove the dough from the bag and deflate ("punch down") thoroughly. Form into one large or two smaller loaves and place in greased loaf pan(s). (A pullman pan makes a nice shape--see the Semolina-Sour Cream Bread recipe.) Cover with oiled or sprayed plastic wrap and allow to rise until the dough is just above the top of the pan.

While the loaves are rising preheat the oven to 375º. When ready to bake you may, if you like, gently brush beaten whole egg over the tops of the loaves for a brown and shiny look. Do *not* do this if you are using a pullman pan with its lid--the dough might stick to the lid! Bake until golden on top, about 40 minutes for two smaller loaves or 50 to 60 minutes for one large loaf. An instant read thermometer should register at least 180º when inserted into the center of the loaf. Remove from the pan and cool on a rack.

ASSORTED TEA SANDWICHES

The bread for these could very well be any of Dan's homemade, but it could also be the very thinly sliced "cocktail" varieties available in most supermarkets. These are some examples of dainty sandwiches suitable for a tea, but I urge you to use your imagination and to be creative with other combinations, too!

In a food processor fitted with the metal blade process the cheese and butter until they are well blended, about 30 seconds. Scrape down the workbowl if necessary with a rubber spatula.

Spread this mixture thinly on each slice of bread. Cut each slice into 4 triangles and place small sprigs of watercress on half the triangles; cover with the remaining triangles. Serve immediately or cover with a lightly dampened tea towel and refrigerate up to 2 hours.

Spread the mayonnaise or butter thinly on each slice of bread. Cut each slice into 4 squares. Place a slice of avocado and egg on each square, then top with a scant 1/4 teaspoon of caviar. Serve immediately.

OTHER SUGGESTIONS INCLUDE:

- English cucumbers with herbed cream cheese.
- Fresh mozzarella cheese, sliced, with ripe plum tomatoes and fresh basil.
- Ripe brie cheese, thinly sliced Black Forest ham and dijon mustard with green peppercorns.

This is a wonderful yeast bread flavored with cocoa and ground pecans and filled with brown sugar, chocolate, butter and more pecans! If the idea of a chocolate "bread" puts you off just think of it as a coffee cake!

DOUGH

3/4 cup milk

1/3 cup brown sugar

1 tablespoon active dry yeast

1 large egg

3 cups pastry flour or all purpose unbleached flour, approximately

3/4 cup unsweetened cocoa

1 teaspoon kosher salt

3/4 cup pecan pieces

6 tablespoons unsalted butter, at room temperature

FILLING

2/3 cup brown sugar

Zest of 1 orange

1 1/3 cups pecan pieces

6 tablespoons unsalted butter

2 ounces semisweet chocolate

1/2 teaspoon almond extract

CHOCOLATE PECAN RING LOAF

Heat the milk to 105º to 115º. Stir in the brown sugar and the yeast and allow to stand for about 5 minutes, until the mixture is foamy. Stir in the egg, mixing well.

If you are making the dough in a food processor (a machine with a flour capacity of at least 6 cups will work best) place the flour, cocoa, salt, and pecans in the workbowl fitted with the metal blade. Run the machine until the nuts have been ground into the flour. Add the butter and run the machine for about 20 seconds, until the butter has disappeared into the flour. Remove the metal blade and insert the dough blade if so equipped.

Stir the yeast mixture and with the machine running pour it into the workbowl as quickly as the flour absorbs it. If you hear "sloshing" you are pouring too quickly. Allow the dough ball to form and rotate inside the machine for 30 seconds, adding a little flour if necessary to prevent the dough from sticking to the workbowl.

If you are using a mixer, place the liquids in the bowl and fit the machine with the pastry paddle to speed the dough formation. Grind or chop the pecans quite finely. Melt the butter and add it to the liquids in the bowl. Add the salt, pecans, cocoa and about 1/2 the flour in the mixer bowl and run on low speed until a batter has formed. Remove the pastry paddle, insert the dough hook and continue running the mixer while adding flour until a dough ball forms. Continue kneading for about 3 minutes. The dough should just barely clean the sides of the bowl.

Place the dough in a gallon-size plastic bag. Squeeze out all the air and place a wire twist at the *top* of the bag so that the dough has room to expand. Allow it to rise at room temperature until it has doubled in size.

To make the filling place the brown sugar and orange zest in a food processor fitted with the metal blade. Run the machine until the zest is finely chopped, about 10 seconds. Add the pecans and run the machine until they are medium to finely chopped. In a small saucepan melt together the butter and chocolate. Stir in the sugar-nut mixture, then the almond extract.

Remove the dough from the bag. Deflate the dough and roll it into a rectangle about 15x8 inches. Using your hands or a rubber spatula spread the filling over the dough, leaving a 1 inch space along one long side. Moisten that space with a little water or beaten egg, then roll up the dough from the opposite side toward the moistened strip. Pinch the seam tightly and squeeze the dough gently with your hands until it is a uniform rope shape. Bring the ends together to form a ring, sealing them with a little water or beaten egg. Place the dough into a large, greased Bundt pan or other ring mold. Cover with oiled plastic wrap and allow to rise until nearly doubled in size.

GLAZE

3 ounces semisweet chocolate

2 tablespoons sugar

2 tablespoons water

2 tablespoons butter

Preheat the oven to 350º. Remove the plastic wrap and bake the bread 35 to 45 minutes, until an instant read thermometer registers 180º. Invert the pan over a cooling rack and remove the bread from the pan. Cool on the rack.

Make the glaze by melting together the chocolate, sugar and water. Remove from the heat and stir in the butter. Drizzle over the bread.

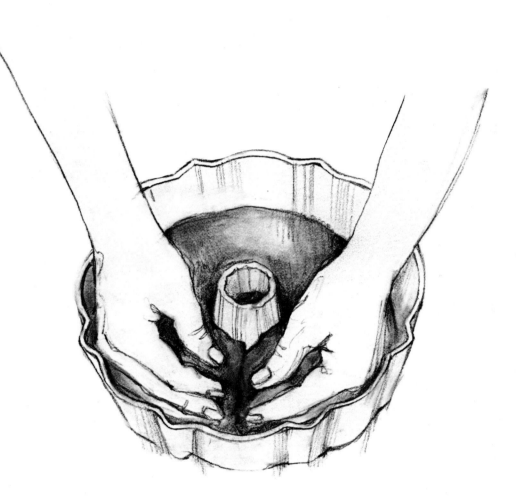

Green-Pea Soup with Basil
Stuffed Breast of Veal
Chili-Pepper Pasta Salad
Minty-Yogurt Salad
Rich Strawberry Ice Cream

DINNER
WHEN IT SIZZLES

hat to do on those summer nights when it is just too hot to cook? Plan ahead! Clever cooks rise early and do the bulk of their preparation in the cooler hours of the morning. So later, at the appointed hour, the happy cook need only assemble and garnish foods which have been mostly prepared in advance!

Our menu for "Dinner When it Sizzles" is an ambitious one. Feel free to choose only some parts of it for a small and informal gathering, or prepare the entire menu for a larger group. Or maybe even better, do what we did during the recipe testing for this book--delegate some of the cooking to your invited guests! Everything we have included in our menu can be made up to two days in advance; the salads can be prepared up to the point of assembly and tossed together at the last minute.

Dan's cool Green-Pea Soup with Basil is a refreshing and colorful appetizer, bursting with flavor and the heady scent of fresh basil. Such fresh herbs are now widely available in better supermarkets. They are also very easy to grow either outside or inside your kitchen window.

The main course is a boneless Breast of Veal rolled around a savory stuffing, served chilled and thinly sliced. It reminds me of summer Italian cooking--it is a light meat dish but is hearty enough to satisfy a good appetite on a sizzling summer evening. It also makes great leftovers for a few more hot-weather meals.

Kathleen offers a spicy Chili-Pepper Pasta Salad as a zesty accompaniment. Virtually a meal in itself, this salad is an exciting combination of flavors and textures. Fresh pasta is no longer difficult to get; buy it at local delicatessens or specialty groceries if you would rather not make it yourself.

Georgia suggests her Minty-Yogurt Salad to complement our meal. It is low in calories, high in flavor and includes a variety of crisp vegetables.

Summer would not be the same without homemade ice cream. Diane's Rich Strawberry Ice Cream is one of the best we have ever eaten! It is easily made using any of the various ice cream makers now on the market.

So remember: plan ahead, then relax, enjoy and eat well during summer's dog days!

Audrey L. Brownson

GREEN-PEA SOUP WITH BASIL

2 pounds frozen green peas, thawed but not warm

2 10-ounce cans chicken broth

1 cup plain yogurt

2 teaspoons sherry vinegar (or use red wine vinegar)

Freshly ground black pepper, to taste

1 teaspoon freshly grated nutmeg, or to taste

1 small onion, finely diced

2 medium tomatoes, peeled, seeded and diced 1/4 inch

1 tablespoon kosher salt, or to taste

1 small bunch fresh basil

One afternoon in the spring of 1986 I found myself busy completing the final mowing of the lawn at a house from which Kathleen and I were moving and into which Audrey was about to move. That evening I needed to bring something for the book, a recipe which would complement the other foods. I created this quick and easy soup which was well received and has since become known as Audrey's Lawn Soup! Serve it cold. You may freeze it, but you will lose the brilliant green color if you do.

Purée the peas in the bowl of a blender or food processor, adding stock until it has all been incorporated. Add the yogurt, vinegar, pepper and nutmeg. Process to blend and pour the soup into a mixing bowl. Add the onion and tomato. Remove one of the tiniest basil leaves for each serving, to use as garnish. Thinly slice the remaining leaves and stir into the soup. Taste and adjust seasonings to your liking.

To serve, portion into individual bowls and float the tiny basil leaves on top. Makes 6 to 8 servings.

MINTY-YOGURT SALAD

1 cup tiny raw cauliflowerets

2 cups thinly sliced raw mushrooms

1 cup tiny broccoli flowerets

2 cups cherry tomatoes, halved

1 cup sliced and pitted black olives

DRESSING

1 cup plain yogurt

1/2 cup olive oil

1/4 cup white wine vinegar

1 clove garlic, minced

1/4 cup lemon juice

1/4 cup chopped fresh mint, or 1 tablespoon dried (fresh is best!)

Salt and pepper, to taste

1 small head romaine or leaf lettuce

Here is a ridiculously easy salad, yet it is refreshing and pleasingly crunchy!

Toss the vegetables carefully so as not to mash the tomatoes. Mix the dressing ingredients well and pour over the vegetables, then toss gently again.

Serve in individual dishes lined with lettuce leaves, or line a bowl or platter with lettuce and arrange the salad on top.

STUFFING

2 tablespoons olive oil

2 cloves garlic, finely minced

1 cup minced leeks (white part only), or onions

1 1/2 cups whole-milk ricotta cheese

1/4 cup grated parmesan cheese

2 large eggs, beaten

1/2 cup finely minced parsley

1 teaspoon ground rosemary, or 1 tablespoon chopped fresh

1/2 teaspoon freshly grated nutmeg

Salt and freshly ground black pepper, to taste

2 ounces prosciutto or smoked ham, finely diced

1 breast of veal, 5 to 6 pounds, boned by your butcher

Salt and freshly ground black pepper, to taste

1 cup chicken stock

1/2 cup dry white wine or dry vermouth

1 rib celery, cut in 2 inch pieces

1 carrot, cut in 2 inch pieces

1 well-washed leek, cut in 2 inch pieces (or 1 small onion cut in eighths)

6 sprigs parsley

1 bay leaf

2 tablespoons unsalted butter or olive oil

STUFFED BREAST OF VEAL

Veal breasts vary in size so you may need to adjust the amount of filling according to the size you are able to purchase. Ask the butcher to save the bones for you--they can be the start of a great homemade stock!

This dish could also be served warm on a cold winter night, in which case allow it to stand out of the oven, covered with foil, for at least 30 minutes before slicing. This will give the stuffing a chance to set up.

Preheat the oven to 400º.

Heat the olive oil in a medium saucepan. Gently sauté the garlic and leeks or onions until they are soft but not browned. Set aside to cool slightly.

In a large bowl blend the remaining stuffing ingredients, then stir in the garlic and leeks or onions.

Place the veal breast fat side down on your work surface. Sprinkle lightly with salt and pepper. Spread the filling over the meat, leaving about a 1 inch border on all four sides. Roll up snugly, but not so tightly that the filling oozes out, and secure with kitchen twine.

In a roaster large enough to hold the stuffed roast, place the stock, wine, celery, carrot, leek or onion, parsley and bay leaf. Place the breast on top of all this and dot with the 2 tablespoons butter or oil.

Place in the preheated oven and bake for 1 hour without turning or basting. Reduce the oven to 350º and bake 30 minutes more, basting occasionally. Remove from the oven and let cool in the cooking liquid. Chill at least three hours or overnight before slicing. Serve cold or at room temperature.

FOR CHILI-PEPPER PASTA

1 1/2 cups all purpose unbleached flour

2 tablespoons ground cayenne pepper

1 teaspoon ground cumin

2 large eggs, beaten

Additional flour or water, if needed

CILANTRO PESTO

6 ounces good quality parmesan or other dry grating cheese, cut in 1-inch cubes

2/3 cup walnuts

2 cups fresh cilantro leaves, loosely packed, washed and dried

3/4 cup good quality, extra virgin olive oil

Salt, to taste

SALAD INGREDIENTS

2 ounces jicama, peeled and cut into matchsticks about 1/4 inch by 1 inch

1 red-skinned apple, cored and finely chopped

1 2.2 ounce can sliced black olives

2 ounces shredded smoked cheese (or use crumbled blue cheese)

1 ounce pepperoni, cut into fine shreds

1 head romaine or leaf lettuce

1/3 cup toasted pine nuts

2 ripe, fresh tomatoes, wedged

CHILI-PEPPER PASTA SALAD

Eaten strictly by themselves these would be some pretty spicy noodles, but in concert with Cilantro Pesto and the salad ingredients, these noodles add up to a refreshingly tangy hot weather dish! They can be prepared well in advance, too. If you choose to buy the pasta rather than make it, you will lose the spicing in the noodles, so you would need to add a little cumin and cayenne to the pesto sauce until you like the "bite."

To make the pasta place the flour and spices in the workbowl of a food processor fitted with the metal blade. Run the machine 3 or 4 seconds, then pour the eggs in and run the machine until the dough gathers together in a ball. Add a little water, if necessary, to make it form a ball. It is not necessary to knead the dough in the machine.

Remove the dough from the machine and, if time allows, rest it for 30 minutes, covered. Roll the dough through a hand or electric pasta roller as with any other noodle dough, then cut into fettuccine.

Bring 6 or 7 quarts of water to a boil in a large pot, adding about 1 tablespoon of salt after the water boils. Cook the noodles until they are barely done--not raw tasting but not mushy, probably not over 2 to 3 minutes. Drain and refresh under cold running water, then drain well. If you are not putting the salad together at this point toss the noodles with a 1/4 cup of vegetable oil to prevent sticking and refrigerate them.

To make the cilantro pesto place the cheese in the workbowl of a food processor fitted with the metal blade. Run the machine until the cheese is finely ground (it will make a lot of noise at first) then add the remaining ingredients and process until smooth.

To assemble the salad, toss the noodles with the pesto sauce and the jicama, apple, olives, smoked or blue cheese and pepperoni. Taste for salt and adjust if necessary. Arrange the salad on leaves of romaine or leaf lettuce on a large platter and garnish with the pine nuts and tomatoes. Serve cold or at room temperature.

K. T.

2 pints fresh, or frozen and unsweetened, strawberries
2 tablespoons sugar
1/4 cup Grand Marnier
2 cups milk
1/2 vanilla bean, split lengthwise
1 cup sugar
5 egg yolks
Dash salt
1 cup heavy cream

RICH STRAWBERRY ICE CREAM

Wash, hull and coarsely chop the strawberries. Combine with the sugar and Grand Marnier in a medium bowl. Chill.

In a medium saucepan combine the milk and vanilla bean. Bring the milk just to a simmer and remove from the heat. Cool to room temperature. Remove the vanilla bean and scrape the seeds from the pod into the cooled milk. Reserve.

In the top of a double boiler set over (but not *in*) simmering water, combine the cup of sugar, egg yolks and salt. Whisk to combine, then beat constantly until thick and lemon colored. Add the milk to the egg mixture and cook, stirring constantly, until the mixture coats the back of a spoon like heavy cream. Cool quickly by placing the top of the double boiler into a bowl of ice water and stirring gently.

When the custard is cool add the strawberries and heavy cream. Freeze in an ice cream maker according to the manufacturer's instructions.

Makes about 1 quart.

DM

Kabob Mashwi--Grilled Ground Meat Kabobs
Grilled Chicken with Dan's Barbecue Sauce
Grilled Polenta with Olive and Red Pepper Topping
Ratatouille on a Stick
Peponi Me Ouzo--Marinated Melon
Caramel Brownies

A BARBECUE

t is no secret that Americans love to grill foods outdoors! Some of them even grill *indoors* using one of the rangetop grills provided by several appliance manufacturers. Whether you belong to James Beard's famous "Cremation School of Cookery" or are an accomplished ember tender you can easily stray far beyond the 'burger and 'dog menus of the average household. Grilling is, for the most part, a simple exercise: pick a fuel (wood, charcoal, gas), light the fuel, regulate the heat or height of the grill, add the food, and monitor its progress while inhaling delicious aromas all the while! With a little practice you will learn to control flareups and outmaneuver insistent mosquitoes. Outdoor cooking is just plain fun for many of us! Here is a menu to broaden your grilling horizons. There are a few spices called for but nothing which cannot be easily made at home or picked up ready-made.

Dan Taggart

KABOB MASHWI
(Grilled Ground Meat Kabobs)

These are tasty little ovals of seasoned, finely ground lamb or beef. They are served along with a very simple-to-make but flavorful yogurt-mint sauce.

To make the kabobs mix the meat with the parsley, onion, salt and seasoning. Grind in a food processor until the meat is very fine or knead by hand or in a mixer until a smooth texture results. Moisten your hands with water, take a generous 2 tablespoons of the meat mixture and mold around a *flat* metal skewer. The kabobs should be about 4 inches long with tapered ends. Allow 2 kabobs per skewer. Refrigerate for at least 30 minutes to firm the meat before grilling.

To make the spice mixture which goes in the kabobs, stir together all ingredients and store in a tightly covered jar. Makes about 1/2 cup.

To make the yogurt sauce, stir together all the ingredients and refrigerate several hours.

When ready to serve, brush the kabobs with the olive oil and grill close to the coals for about 5 minutes, turning frequently. Serve with the yogurt sauce.

Ingredients (left column)

1/3 cup olive oil

4 cloves garlic, minced

1 jumbo yellow onion, chopped

2 to 3 jalapeño chili peppers, seeded and minced

1 1/4 cups white or cider vinegar

1 cup water

1 6-ounce can tomato paste

1/4 cup dark molasses

1/2 cup honey

3 tablespoons soy sauce

1 teaspoon dry mustard

1 teaspoon ground cinnamon

1 teaspoon salt

2 tablespoons liquid smoke

Whole or cut up chicken, enough to feed your guests

POLENTA

2 quarts light chicken stock

1 pound yellow cornmeal

PEPPER-OLIVE SAUCE

4 large sweet red peppers

4 ounces Sicilian style green olives, herbed or plain, pitted and coarsely chopped

5 ounces Calamata or other big, black, cured olives, pitted and coarsely chopped

5 tablespoons extra virgin olive oil

1 tablespoon Balsamic vinegar

GRILLED CHICKEN WITH DAN'S BARBECUE SAUCE

During the recipe testing for this book I created two other chicken dishes for this menu. They were both good eating, but after much reflection Kathleen and I decided that the kind of food which would appeal most would be more traditionally American--something, say, with a Southwestern flavor. So I created this barbecue sauce which includes chilies, onions, and tomato, among other ingredients. We have tested the barbecue sauce on grilled hamburgers and pork spareribs, and, believe it or not, we found it appealing on grilled halibut steaks as well. We hope you like it, too!

Heat the olive oil in a medium saucepan. Add the garlic, onion and jalapeños and cook, stirring often, until they are soft but not browned.

Add the other sauce ingredients, bring to a boil, reduce to a simmer and cook, partially covered, for 30 to 40 minutes. Taste and adjust the flavor with more vinegar or salt if necessary. Cool and refrigerate. Keeps several weeks.

Grill the chicken pieces or whole birds in your favorite manner, basting with this sauce only during the last 5 to 10 minutes to prevent the sauce from burning. Brush on more sauce after removing the chicken from the grill.

GRILLED POLENTA WITH OLIVE AND RED PEPPER TOPPING

Polenta--cornmeal loaf--is very popular in Italian cooking. In our menu we grill slices of polenta and top them with an easy-to-make pepper and olive sauce. Be sure to use a good quality extra virgin olive oil, and if you can find it, use Balsamic vinegar. The polenta itself is quite easy to prepare. You will have more than enough for our barbecue menu; try some sauteed in butter and topped with warm maple syrup for breakfast.

To make the polenta bring the chicken stock to a boil in a 4-quart or larger heavy-bottomed saucepan or dutch oven. Reduce to a simmer and add the cornmeal very slowly, stirring constantly. Be careful that it is not boiling too rapidly as it thickens or it could sputter and burn you! Continue to cook and stir for approximately 20 minutes or until the mixture pulls away from the sides of the pan and a wooden spoon will stand upright in it.

6 thick (3/4 to 1 inch) slices polenta

Regular grade olive oil

Turn the polenta into a well-oiled, large bread pan, about 10x4 inches. Pack down well and smooth the top. Allow to cool to room temperature and then cover and refrigerate overnight, or for at least 6 hours. Near serving time loosen the edges of the polenta and turn it out onto a cutting board. Cut a thick slice for each person to be served. Brush the slices with the regular grade of olive oil (extra virgin is a bit pricey to use for cooking, we think) and cook over hot coals until warm and a bit browned. Top with some of the olive sauce.

To make the sauce, char the skins of the peppers over a gas flame or directly on an electric burner set on high. Place the peppers in a plastic bag for a few minutes to "steam," then scrape off the charred skin. Remove the seeds, then cut the peppers into matchstick pieces and combine them with the olives, olive oil and vinegar.

NOTE: Browning the polenta will probably take about 20 minutes.

K. T.

For about 16 skewers:

1 small eggplant

1/2 pound zucchini

1 sweet red pepper

1 large onion

1 pint cherry tomatoes

4 tablespoons olive oil

Juice of 1 lemon

Salt and freshly ground black pepper, to taste

3 cloves garlic, crushed

1/3 cup minced parsley, Italian flat-leaf is best

1 tablespoon herbes de Provence

1/4 cup olive oil

Bamboo or metal skewers

RATATOUILLE ON A STICK

Cut the eggplant in quarters lengthwise and cut into 1/2 inch cubes. Do the same with the zucchini. Cut the pepper into small pieces about 1/2 inch square. Cut the onion in half horizontally, then each half quartered. Separate the onion into small pieces about the size of the other vegetables. Place the vegetables on skewers, placing two pieces of each type of vegetable except the tomatoes, arranging them so that the colors vary. For instance: eggplant, red pepper, zucchini, onion and a cherry tomato. If you use bamboo skewers cut off the excess beyond the vegetables so that the skewers do not burn. Place the skewers in a flat container large enough to hold them--a jelly roll pan works well.

Mix the 4 tablespoons of olive oil, lemon juice, salt and pepper and garlic. Pour the mixture over the vegetables. Sprinkle on the herbs. Refrigerate 4 hours or longer.

Grill over hot coals, brushing with the extra olive oil, until the vegetables are tender, turning once or twice.

NOTE: Thawed frozen pearl onions may be substituted and look nice on these skewers, too.

2 large melons, halved with seeds removed

1/4 cup sugar

2 tablespoons ouzo (a Greek licorice flavored liqueur)

Rind of 1 lime, grated

2 ounces unsweetened chocolate

1 stick (4 ounces) unsalted butter

2 large eggs, beaten

1 cup sugar

1/2 cup all purpose flour

1 teaspoon vanilla extract

1 cup chopped walnuts

CARAMEL FILLING

5 1/2 tablespoons (2 3/4 ounces) unsalted butter

1 cup powdered sugar

1/2 cup heavy cream

1 tablespoon light corn syrup

GLAZE

1 tablespoon unsalted butter

2 ounces semisweet chocolate

PEPONI ME OUZO
(Marinated Melon)

Peel the melons and cut them into 1 inch pieces. Place in a glass serving bowl along with the sugar and ouzo. Allow to stand, uncovered, for at least 3 hours, turning occasionally.

In very hot weather refrigerate the melon for the last hour before serving. Sprinkle the grated lime zest over the fruit before serving.

Serves 8 to 10.

CARAMEL BROWNIES

This recipe was kindly given to me by my cousin, Leslie Lipman. She serves these show stopping brownies cut into 1-inch squares, as they are very rich. These freeze very well.

Preheat the oven to 350º. Line an 8-inch square baking pan with aluminum foil and butter it lightly but evenly.

In a heavy saucepan melt the unsweetened chocolate and 4 ounces of butter over low heat. Stir to combine and remove from the heat when almost melted. Stir until smooth. Slowly add the beaten eggs, stirring constantly. When the eggs are well-combined, add the sugar, flour, vanilla and walnuts, mixing well after each addition. Turn into the prepared pan and smooth the top. Bake in the middle of the preheated oven 20 to 25 minutes. Cool in the pan on a rack.

While the brownies are cooling make the filling. Combine the 5 1/2 tablespoons of butter, powdered sugar, cream and corn syrup in a heavy saucepan. Bring to a boil slowly over medium heat. Do *not* stir at any point! Let the mixture boil until it reaches 220-225º on a candy thermometer. Remove from the heat and spread immediately over the cooled brownies. Allow to cool until the filling is set.

When the caramel is no longer tacky to the touch, make the glaze. In the top of a double boiler melt the one tablespoon of butter and 2 ounces of semisweet chocolate over barely simmering water. Blend until smooth and spread evenly over the cooled filling.

To cut the brownies invert the pan over a large plate or other flat surface. Remove the pan and peel off the foil. Invert the brownies again, to right side up, and cut into squares with a heavy, sharp knife. Makes about 64 1-inch squares or 16 2-inch squares.

Chilled Pumpkin Soup with Green Chilies
Sautéed Chicken with Tarragon and Lime
Myla Me Moshato--Apples in Muscatel

Cold Beet Soup
Sauté of Pork with Rosemary Mustard Sauce
Fancy Yogurt in a Chocolate Cup

Asparagus with a Sherry Vinegar/Mustard Vinaigrette
Fillets of Red Snapper with Spicy Tomato Sauce
Fresh Strawberries in Balsamic Vinegar

---◆---

DINNER IN AN HOUR

egardless of whether we are casual cooks or dedicated ones, we are all in a position at times when we would like to entertain but simply do not have the pleasure of spending all day in the kitchen. These are times to have a few tricks up your sleeve, so that you can produce something both simple and elegant.

We offer three separate menus for the short-order entertainer! All the ingredients should be readily available in a well-stocked grocery, leaving at most one additional stop at your butcher or fish market.

Our first menu begins with a lovely Chilled Pumpkin Soup. It is a snap to make and the appearance and taste are sensational. Your guests will never know it took you only ten minutes to make! Follow the soup with Sautéed Chicken Breasts with Tarragon and Lime. They can be sautéed after the soup is served or done ahead and held in a 200º oven for up to 20 minutes. You could accompany the chicken with a simply prepared fresh vegetable or just add a fresh garnish to the plate. Apples in Muscatel, created by Georgia, have become a favorite of mine; it is a great recipe to have up your sleeve.

Our second menu also begins with a soup. It is made from beets, is a beautiful pink color and is served cold! It whizzes together in a blender. Dan offers a lovely Sauté of Pork Tenderloin with a Rosemary Mustard Sauce. Again, this entrée can stand on its own or be served with a vegetable of choice. If asparagus is in season splurge and serve only the tips, lightly steamed! Begin the menu by preparing Kathleen's dessert first; it uses good quality frozen yogurt and adds the wonderful enhancements of raisins, scotch and hazelnuts. Chocolate shells add an elegant touch, but if you cannot find them just serve this dessert in your prettiest dessert bowls. No one would complain if you offered a chocolate truffle to accompany!

Finally, we suggest an elegant but easy menu with fish as the entrée. Audrey created a wonderful oven-baked recipe--Fillets of Red Snapper in a Spicy Tomato Sauce. If you wish, accompany it with rice or pasta. While the fish is baking you can serve your salad as a first course. Specialty vinegars are appearing in greater numbers in our supermarkets and sherry vinegar is a favorite of mine. It is used here to make a vinaigrette dressing which is poured over lightly cooked and chilled asparagus--always a delightful beginning to any meal. Speaking of vinegars, I was quite pleasantly surprised when I tasted Audrey's Strawberries in Balsamic Vinegar--you will be too!

With these three menus added to your repertoire you are ready to take on Dinner in An Hour with ease and confidence! Spend your extra time perusing the other sections of the cookbook for more elaborate entertaining.

Diane J Morgan

To serve 6:

1 16-ounce can plain pumpkin

2 cups chicken stock

3/4 cup buttermilk

1 3-1/2 ounce can diced mild green chilies

1 teaspoon sugar

1/4 teaspoon ground cinnamon

Salt to taste

1/4 cup dry gin (optional)

1/2 cup chopped toasted almonds, as garnish

Plain yogurt, as garnish

CHILLED PUMPKIN SOUP WITH GREEN CHILIES

I adore cold soup all year round, but especially in the summertime, of course. My pumpkin soup represents the height of speed and simplicity. It was one of the most difficult recipes to perfect in the book. I just would not give up on the idea and I believe the result is worth the effort!

Mix all soup ingredients in a large mixing bowl using a whisk. Cover and refrigerate until ready to serve. Adjust the seasonings while cold, before serving.

When ready to serve ladle into bowls. Place a dollop of yogurt on each portion and sprinkle with some toasted almonds.

K. T.

To serve 6:

3 whole or 6 half chicken breasts, skinned and boned

2 eggs

1 cup flour

1 cup dry bread crumbs

1 1/2 tablespoons dried tarragon leaves, crushed

1 1/2 teaspoons kosher salt

Freshly ground black pepper, to taste

1 teaspoon sugar

SAUTÉED CHICKEN WITH TARRAGON AND LIME

Trim the chicken of excess fat or tendons. Split the breasts if they are whole, by removing the cartilage in the center. Pull the tenderloins from each side (the extra piece of flesh at the top of each breast half) and remove the tendon in the tenderloin by holding a knife blade perpendicular against the meat while pulling the tendon away from the meat. Use the tenderloins for this meal or save them for another.

On a work surface place a long piece of plastic wrap. Place the chicken pieces on it, then cover with another piece of plastic wrap. Using a flat (non-serrated) meat pounder or the bottom of a pan pound the chicken into uniformly thin pieces without tearing the meat.

Place the flour on a large dinner plate. Combine the crumbs, tarragon, salt, pepper and sugar on another large plate. Beat the eggs in a shallow, wide bowl.

4 to 6 tablespoons olive oil

4 to 6 tablespoons butter

2 limes, cut into wedges

Have two cookie sheets handy. Dip each chicken piece first in the flour, then in the egg and finally into the crumb mixture. Place them on the cookie sheets until you are ready to cook them. You may do this as much as 30 minutes in advance.

Heat half the olive oil in a large sauté pan. When hot add half the butter and swirl to coat the pan. Add three or more chicken pieces to the pan without crowding and sauté them for 1 to 2 minutes per side over medium high heat until they are crisp and golden. Do not overcook them. Sauté the remaining chicken in the same manner adding more olive oil and butter to the pan as needed. Serve hot with wedges of lime to accompany the chicken.

DM

---

6 tart cooking apples, such as Newton or Granny Smith

4 tablespoons (2 ounces) unsalted butter

1/4 cup light brown sugar

1/2 cup muscatel wine, or other dark, sweet wine

Sprinkle of cinnamon and nutmeg

Whipped cream, sweetened

MYLA ME MOSHATO
(Apples in Muscatel)

Peel and core the apples and slice them thinly and uniformly.

Melt the butter in a large sauté pan. Add the apples and cook over moderate heat, turning the apples to cook them on both sides. Sprinkle them with the sugar. Cover the pan and simmer for 5 minutes, then uncover the pan, add the wine and cook over low heat until the apples are cooked, shaking the pan occasionally. The apples should not be mushy, but the sauce should thicken. Sprinkle a little cinnamon and nutmeg over the apples near the end of the cooking.

Serve warm, accompanied by sweetened whipped cream or vanilla ice cream.

COLD BEET SOUP

1/2 cup ice-cold water

1 8-ounce can pickled beets, drained

1 teaspoon kosher salt

Freshly ground black pepper, to taste

1 small onion, peeled, ends discarded, quartered

1 (1/2x2-inch) piece lemon peel

1 cup homemade or canned chicken stock

1 1/2 to 2 teaspoons prepared horseradish

1 1/2 cups sour cream

I like to serve this soup ungarnished in black china soup bowls to highlight its beautiful color. It is also quite attractive in glass soup bowls garnished with a couple of julienned pieces of pickled beet or a small spoonful of sour cream floating in the center.

Put the water, beets, salt, pepper, onion, lemon peel and half the stock into a blender container. Purée this mixture, then add the remaining stock, the horseradish and sour cream and blend thoroughly. Taste and adjust seasonings.

Serve immediately or refrigerate until ready to serve.

DM

SAUTÉ OF PORK WITH ROSEMARY MUSTARD SAUCE

This is a quick and delicious dish using tenderloin of pork, a cut of meat overlooked by many cooks. Like beef it is exceedingly tender but a bit lighter in flavor.

2 pork tenderloins (about 1 to 1 1/2 pounds total) trimmed of gristle

Clarified butter or vegetable oil

1/4 cup dry vermouth or dry white wine

1 cup homemade or canned chicken stock

1 1/2 tablespoons dijon mustard

1 teaspoon dried rosemary, crushed or ground in a spice mill, or 1 tablespoon chopped fresh

1 cup heavy cream

Salt and freshly ground black pepper, to taste

Slice the pork on the diagonal (so that the slices are larger) about 1/2 to 3/4 inch thick. Lay the slices on a sheet of plastic wrap. Cover with another sheet of plastic wrap and use a flat meat pounder or the bottom of a pan to pound the pork to a uniform thickness of about 1/4 inch.

Heat a large, heavy skillet or griddle until very hot. Add 3 to 4 tablespoons of clarified butter or vegetable oil, then sauté the pork slices so that they brown quickly on both sides. This should take about 1 minute per side. Remove the pork slices to a platter in a barely warm oven.

To the pan add the vermouth or wine, scraping any browned bits from the bottom. Add the stock, mustard and rosemary and cook over medium high heat until the stock is reduced to less than 1/2 cup. Add the cream and continue to boil until the sauce is thickened to your liking. Taste for salt and pepper. Pour the sauce over the pork and serve immediately.

1/3 cup raisins

1/2 cup scotch whisky

1 pint vanilla frozen yogurt

1/3 cup whole toasted hazelnuts

6 chocolate shells

FANCY YOGURT IN A CHOCOLATE CUP

Soak the raisins in the whisky for about 10 minutes. Drain, saving the whisky.

Place the frozen yogurt in the workbowl of a food processor fitted with the metal blade. Pulse a few times to lighten the texture. Sprinkle the raisins and hazelnuts evenly over the yogurt and pulse the machine just to mix the ingredients without chopping them. Repack the yogurt into a container and freeze until ready to serve.

To serve, portion the yogurt into the chocolate shells. Spoon some of the reserved scotch over the yogurt if you like. Serve immediately!

K. T.

36 spears of asparagus (allow 6 per person)

VINAIGRETTE

1 small clove garlic

1/2 teaspoon kosher salt

1 teaspoon sugar

Freshly ground black pepper, to taste

1 teaspoon dijon mustard

2 tablespoons sherry vinegar

6 tablespoons olive oil

2 tablespoons heavy cream

1 tablespoon chopped fresh chervil, or 1 teaspoon dried plus 1 teaspoon freshly minced parsley

ASPARAGUS WITH A SHERRY VINEGAR/MUSTARD VINAIGRETTE

Cut the tough ends from the asparagus and peel the stalks from just below the tip to the base; a vegetable peeler does a good job of this, or there are special asparagus peelers sold just for the job. Bring a large pan of salted water to a rolling boil, add the asparagus and cook for 2 to 4 minutes. The asparagus should be a brilliant green and be just tender but not mushy. Immediately remove from the boiling water and plunge into a bowl of ice water to stop the cooking. Drain well on paper towels and reserve.

In a jar with a tight-fitting lid, crush the garlic using a garlic press (or finely mince it using a chef's knife) and add the remaining dressing ingredients. Shake the jar to thoroughly mix the dressing, then taste it. Adjust the seasonings, if necessary, and taste again. Reserve.

When ready to serve, place six prepared asparagus spears on each serving plate and spoon some of the well-shaken dressing over the top. Garnish with some fresh chervil leaves if available. Serve at room temperature.

DM

3 tablespoons olive oil

1/3 cup finely chopped onion

1 clove garlic, finely minced

1 shallot, finely minced

3 cups canned plum tomatoes, drained, seeded and coarsely chopped

3 tablespoons tomato paste

1 teaspoon thyme

1/4 teaspoon ground fennel

1/8 teaspoon cayenne pepper

2 tablespoons minced fresh parsley

Salt and pepper, to taste

6 6-ounce red snapper fillets

FILLETS OF RED SNAPPER WITH SPICY TOMATO SAUCE

Preheat the oven to 425°. Heat the oil in a heavy saucepan. Cook the onions, garlic and shallot over medium heat until soft but not browned.

Add the remaining seven sauce ingredients, stir to blend, then simmer for 10 minutes. Taste and adjust seasonings.

Oil a baking dish large enough to accomodate the fish in a single layer. Arrange the fillets in the dish. Pour the sauce over the fish and bake in the preheated oven for 15 to 20 minutes or until the fish is no longer translucent and the sauce is bubbling.

Serve with rice or pasta.

To serve 6:

2 pints fresh strawberries

1/4 cup brown sugar

2 to 4 tablespoons balsamic vinegar (a dark colored, aged and very mellow vinegar available in specialty stores and some supermarkets)

FRESH STRAWBERRIES IN BALSAMIC VINEGAR

Stem and halve the strawberries. Toss with the brown sugar and vinegar to taste. Garnish with mint leaves, if available.

Chicken and Artichoke Fricassee
Rice Pilaf with Aromatic Spices
Baby Carrots with Herbs
Cole Slaw with Dill Mayonnaise
Coconut Cake with Jam Filling and Chocolate Glaze

———————————◆———————————

A FAMILY GATHERING

A family gathering is always a special time. It seems especially so these days when the pace of life keeps us from getting together as often as we would like, even if we live in the same city!! When I am in the company of loved ones I prefer to serve a meal which can be prepared ahead of time. Last minute completion is quick and simple, easily accomplished while my family relaxes and visits over a glass of wine or beer. This is just such a meal.

The Chicken and Artichoke Fricassee is easily prepared ahead; just before serving it is reheated and the sauce prepared. I have used thickened yogurt to make a tangy, creamy gravy which is lower in fat than the traditional Greek egg-lemon sauce which usually tops this dish. Diane's Rice Pilaf is definitely and deliciously Eastern in flavor--a wonderful foil for the chicken. The accompanying Cole Slaw with Dill Mayonnaise and the Herbed Carrots add lovely bright colors to the plate. Surprisingly, this combination of subtle herbs and spices all blend together on the palate when eaten; they do not "fight" each other at all!!

Kathleen's Coconut Cake with Jam Filling and light Chocolate Glaze is sure to become a favorite of *your* family.

Georgia M. Vareldzis

**6 to 8 fresh "baby" artichokes, or
1 can artichoke hearts**

1 lemon

**6 to 8 small whole potatoes, or
3 to 4 quartered large potatoes,
peeled (optional)**

1 stick (4 ounces) unsalted butter

**1 cut-up frying chicken or 6 to 8
chicken pieces**

Salt and pepper, to taste

1 small bunch green onions, chopped

1 cup dry white wine

**1 tablespoon chopped fresh dill, or
1 teaspoon dried**

1 cup plain yogurt

1 tablespoon flour

CHICKEN AND ARTICHOKE FRICASSEE

Preheat oven to 350⁰. Prepare the fresh artichokes by bending back the lower, outer petals until they snap off. With a serrated knife cut off the artichoke tops about 1/3 of the way down. Cut off the stems. Trim the base and rub all surfaces with a cut lemon half. Cook the artichokes in boiling water to which you have added the remaining juice in the lemon half. Cook about 10 minutes or until they are tender when pierced with a fork in the base. Drain. Canned artichokes need only rinsing; no cooking is required.

Arrange the artichokes and potatoes, if you use them, in a buttered 2 1/2 quart casserole.

Brown the chicken pieces in the butter in a large skillet until they are well-browned on both sides, about 15 minutes. Season with salt and pepper to taste. Arrange the chicken pieces over the vegetables in the casserole.

Cook the green onions in the pan drippings until they are soft. Add the wine and cook until it has reduced by half. Pour the pan juices over the chicken pieces in the casserole and sprinkle the dill over the top.

Cover the casserole and bake in a preheated oven for about 45 minutes, or until the chicken pieces register 180⁰ on an instant read thermometer. Remove the chicken and vegetables to a warmed platter.

Combine the yogurt and flour, then add to the drippings in the casserole and cook over low heat, stirring constantly. *Do not allow the sauce to boil.* Pour the sauce over the chicken and vegetables on the platter, or return them to the casserole and top with the sauce. Serve immediately.

NOTE: If you use small chicken pieces such as separated legs or thighs, or boneless breast pieces, they will cook more quickly than larger cuts. In this case, you may need to bake the casserole for only about 25 minutes, and the potatoes will need to be precooked until they are not quite tender, before placing them in the casserole.

**4 cups chicken stock, preferably
homemade**

1 piece cinnamon stick, 1 inch long

4 whole cloves

RICE PILAF WITH AROMATIC SPICES

Place the chicken stock in a medium saucepan. Combine the next 7 ingredients in a cheesecloth bag and tie securely. Add the bag of spices to the stock and bring to a boil. Reduce to a simmer, cover and cook for 30 minutes. Remove the spice bag, squeeze out its liquid using the back of a spoon and continue simmering the broth--uncovered--until it has reduced to 3 cups.

1 1/2 teaspoons cumin seeds

1 1/2 teaspoons coriander seeds

1 1/2 teaspoons fennel seeds

4 cardamom pods, cracked

1 small onion, peeled and halved

2 cups basmati rice, or other long-grain white rice

1 large onion, peeled, ends removed, quartered

3 cloves garlic

3 quarter-size slices fresh ginger root

6 tablespoons peanut or vegetable oil

2 teaspoons kosher salt

1 1/2 teaspoons ground cumin

1 1/2 teaspoons ground coriander

In the meantime, wash the rice in several changes of cold water until the water runs clear. Drain, then soak the rice in 3 cups fresh cold water for 30 to 40 minutes. Drain thoroughly.

Preheat the oven to 325º. In the workbowl of a food processor fitted with the metal blade, mince the onion, garlic and ginger together by pulsing the machine.

In a shallow, flameproof 2 to 3 quart casserole, heat the oil over moderate heat. Add the minced onion mixture and sauté until it becomes golden and translucent, but do not brown. Add the rice, salt, cumin and coriander and continue to sauté for 6 minutes, stirring constantly. Lower the heat if the rice begins to stick. The rice will turn white.

Add the reduced broth, bring to a simmer and continue to cook until all the broth on the surface of the rice disappears and small air holes form, about 5 minutes. Cover with a tight-fitting lid and place in the preheated oven for 15 to 20 minutes, or until the rice is tender but still slightly firm.

Serve immediately or keep warm until ready to serve. The rice reheats well, either covered in the microwave or in a 250º oven.

DM

To serve 6:

2 pounds baby carrots, scrubbed and ends trimmed

3 tablespoons olive oil

Salt and freshly ground black pepper, to taste

1 tablespoon minced fresh parsley

1 tablespoon minced fresh tarragon, or 1 teaspoon dried

2 tablespoons freshly squeezed lemon juice

BABY CARROTS WITH HERBS

Blanch the carrots in boiling salted water 3 to 4 minutes, or until just barely cooked. Drain and refresh under cold running water to stop the cooking.

In a large skillet heat the olive oil over medium heat. Add the carrots and stir fry briefly to coat them with oil. After 3 to 4 minutes they should be heated through.

Remove the pan from the heat. Season with salt and pepper, add the herbs and lemon juice and toss to mix. Turn into a heated serving bowl.

1 to 1 1/4 pounds white cabbage, quartered, core removed

1 small onion, about 3 ounces, peeled and halved vertically

Salt and freshly ground black pepper, to taste

About 3/4 cup homemade dill mayonnaise

FOR THE MAYONNAISE

1 large whole egg

1 egg yolk

2 tablespoons dijon mustard

2 tablespoons rice or white wine vinegar

1 teaspoon kosher salt

1 1/2 cups vegetable oil

1 tablespoon sugar

1 teaspoon dried dill weed, or 1 tablespoon fresh

COLE SLAW WITH DILL MAYONNAISE

Shred the cabbage into long, thin strips using a sharp knife or a thin disc of a food processor. Thinly slice the onion. Place the vegetables in a large bowl.

Make the mayonnaise by placing the egg, egg yolk, mustard, vinegar and salt in the workbowl of a food processor or a blender container. Run the machine for 5 to 10 seconds, then begin adding the oil in a thin stream. As the mayonnaise thickens the oil may be added a little faster, until all the oil has been absorbed. Add the sugar and dill and run the machine a few more seconds. Taste for seasonings and adjust with salt, pepper or vinegar, as you like. Store covered in the refrigerator; keeps for 10 days or more. (Never use a cracked egg to make mayonnaise, as it could contain bacteria, which might cause illness, since the egg is not cooked.)

Add about 1/2 cup of the mayonnaise and some salt and pepper to the vegetables. Using your very clean hands or two rubber spatulas toss the salad until well mixed, adding more mayonnaise if necessary, to coat the vegetables thoroughly.

Taste for salt and pepper and dill. Adjust if necessary. Chill thoroughly before serving.

COCONUT CAKE WITH JAM FILLING AND CHOCOLATE GLAZE

I think that there is nothing as appropriate for a traditional family meal as a luscious, moist cake! This one is lovely. It is a rich coconut pound cake that is split and filled with berry preserves and then drizzled with a shiny chocolate glaze. It freezes beautifully, so you may prepare it well in advance.

Preheat the oven to 350^0. Butter or spray an 8-cup tube pan.

Sift together the flour, salt, baking soda, baking powder and mace, then set aside. Cream the butter and sugar. Add the eggs one at a time, mixing well after each addition. Add 1/3 of the dry ingredients, then 1/2 of the buttermilk, then 1/3 more of the dry ingredients, then the remaining buttermilk, then the remaining dry ingredients. In each instance, beat just to combine. Stir in the coconut.

Transfer the batter to the prepared pan and smooth the top. Bake in a preheated oven until a tester comes out dry, about 55 to 60 minutes. If you use a shallower pan begin to test for doneness at 45 minutes. Allow the cake to cool in the pan for 10 to 15 minutes, then loosen around the edges and invert onto a cooling rack. Turn right side up and cool completely.

Split the cake in half horizontally with a long-bladed serrated knife and carefully remove the top. Spread the jam on the bottom half, not quite out to the edges. Carefully reposition the top.

Make the glaze by placing the chocolate and water in a heavy saucepan over low heat, or in the top of a double boiler over simmering water. Stir until melted and smooth. Set aside to cool slightly, then drizzle over the cake in a random pattern. The cake should sit for a couple of hours to allow the glaze to set before serving. Serves 12.

K. T.

Fruites de Saison
Savory Mushroom Tart with Poppyseed/Buckwheat Crust
Torta Rustica
Homemade Pork Sausage Patties
Apricot-Banana-Ginger Bread

A LAZY
SUMMER SUNDAY
BRUNCH

ummer days and Sunday mornings have something in common. They can be long, lazy and luxurious. We suggest combining the two--summer and Sunday morning--and inviting a few friends over to enjoy entertaining at a leisurely pace!

As usual, we have tried to design a menu with lots of advance preparation possibilities. Georgia begins our meal with a lovely fruit mélange, the majority of which can be readied the night before. The sherry and ginger can be added in advance, leaving the bananas to add before serving.

Diane's aromatic sweet bread with bananas, apricots and ginger freezes nicely so that it may be baked a week or more in advance. In fact, it is a wonderful bread to have languishing in the freezer on general principles! Audrey and I have each offered an entrée for this menu, as we did for the other brunch menu. For a truly leisurely morning, pick one of them; for a more impressive table (and using another pair of hands, maybe!) go for broke--make both the Savory Mushroom Tart in Poppyseed/Buckwheat Crust and our layered omelette version of a Torta Rustica! The tart's pastry shell could be made a couple of weeks in advance and frozen, the filling could be readied a couple of days ahead, then bake the tart the morning of the brunch. Most of Audrey's Torta Rustica can be prepared the day before, leaving the rolling of the dough, the layering and the baking for Sunday morning. We found that it reheats nicely, too, so you could really finish it completely a day in advance! Likewise, Dan's sausage patties will only benefit from being mixed a day or two before cooking. They are fresh and beautifully seasoned with herbs and not at all hard to make.

So bring lots of summer flowers to the table, as well as your most colorful serving pieces, to appreciate the company of friends and the warmth of the morning!

Kathleen Taggart

3 cups melon balls from cantaloupe, honeydew, watermelon, casaba, etc.
1 cup fresh berries
2 cups pineapple chunks, fresh or canned
1 cup white seedless grapes
1 cup red or blue seedless grapes
1 banana, split lengthwise and cut into 1/4-inch slices
1 cup cream sherry
1/2 teaspoon ground ginger
1/2 cup orange juice, used only if you use fresh pineapple and do not have sufficient juice

FRUITES DE SAISON

This first-course fruit salad is very flexible as to the ingredients. It is really "fruits in season." All kinds of melons can be used for the melon balls, and use whatever berries are "in" at the time! If you cannot get good, sweet, fresh pineapple, I advise you to use chunk pineapple canned in its own juice. The juice acts like lemon juice to keep the fruit from turning dark and makes some liquid in the dish. I suggest serving the fruit in some sort of stemware--a parfait glass, a champagne "saucer" or a stemmed glass dessert dish. This type of presentation shows off the lovely rainbow colors of the fruit, which is half the pleasure of this dish! Two tips: if you add bananas, do so at the last minute because their texture changes if they stay in the juice very long. Also, do not overmix if you add strawberries, since they "bleed" into the salad.

Wash the berries and remove the stems, if attached. Wash the grapes and remove their stems.

Mix all the fruits (except the bananas, if you are working in advance) with the sherry and ginger. Cover and refrigerate until serving.

1 1/2 pounds boneless fresh pork shoulder, not closely trimmed, cut into 1 inch cubes, well chilled
1 tablespoon kosher salt
1 1/2 teaspoons ground sage
1/2 teaspoon dried thyme leaves
1/2 teaspoon Tabasco pepper sauce
1 teaspoon freshly ground black pepper
2 pinches ground allspice

HOMEMADE PORK SAUSAGE PATTIES

Making you own sausage is really no great chore! Here is an easy to make and mildly seasoned sausage, suitable for breakfast use. The use of pork shoulder, which contains an almost perfect marbling of fat, makes getting a moist but not too fatty sausage easy. You might like a little more pork fat in your sausage, but as a group we liked this style.

In the workbowl of a food processor fitted with the metal blade, place all of the pork, if your machine is large enough; otherwise, chop the meat in two batches. Pulse the machine to chop the pork into coarse pieces. Sprinkle the seasonings over the meat and continue to pulse until the sausage is the texture you prefer. Form into a log on a piece of plastic wrap, wrap tightly and refrigerate 12 hours or more to allow best flavor development. You may freeze the sausage, of course.

An alternate method calls for grinding the meat in a hand- or machine-powered meat grinder using a fine plate, then mixing the seasonings in by hand.

To cook, cut the log into pieces about 3/4- to 1-inch thick and sauté in a medium skillet or griddle until they are well-browned on both sides.

FOR THE PASTRY

1/2 cup buckwheat flour
(sold in health-food stores)

2 cups all purpose unbleached flour

2 tablespoons poppyseeds

8 ounces unsalted butter, cut into 16
pieces, frozen

1/2 teaspoon kosher salt

1/2 cup ice water

1 whole egg, for glaze

FOR THE FILLING

1/2 ounce imported dried porcini
mushrooms

1 tablespoon unsalted butter

1/2 pound fresh mushrooms, sliced

1/2 medium onion, sliced

2 tablespoons chopped fresh sage,
 or 2 teaspoons dried

3 large eggs

1 1/4 cups heavy cream

1/2 teaspoon kosher salt

1/4 pound goat cheese

SAVORY MUSHROOM TART WITH POPPYSEED/BUCKWHEAT CRUST

This is a wonderful tart bursting with distinct and earthy flavors. Porcinis, used in the filling, are dried, imported Italian mushrooms with an intense flavor. If you cannot find them at specialty shops, substitute dried domestic mushrooms. Remember to rinse dried mushrooms very well after soaking to remove the sand, which otherwise can spoil the dish!

Like any tart shell, the dough can be mixed, rolled out and frozen in the pan, in advance. The filling can be made ahead. On the day of serving, crumble the goat cheese into the prepared shell, add the custard, and bake.

To make the pastry, place both flours, the poppyseeds, butter and salt in the workbowl of a food processor fitted with the metal blade. Pulse the machine until the mixture resembles coarse meal. With the machine running, pour the water through the feed tube, processing only until the mixture is thoroughly moistened. *Do not let it form a ball.*

Remove the dough to a floured work surface and pat it together to form a disc. You may roll it out at this time, or wrap and refrigerate, or freeze it for later use. Roll the dough into a circle about 13 inches in diameter and transfer it to an 11-inch tart pan with a removable bottom. Trim the edges so that a bit of crust rises above the edge of the pan. Prick the bottom all over using a fork. Place a sheet of aluminum foil over the bottom of the pastry shell and fill it with rice, beans or pie weights. Place the crust in the freezer for about 20 minutes until firm.

Meanwhile, preheat the oven to 400°. When the tart shell is firm bake it for 9 minutes; remove the foil and bake for another 9 minutes. Beat the egg well, paint the shell completely with it and bake another 2 to 3 minutes until the glaze has set. Remove from the oven and cool. Reduce oven heat to 350°.

To make the filling, soak the porcinis in warm water for 20 to 30 minutes. While the dried mushrooms are soaking, melt the butter in a 9-to 10-inch sauté pan and cook the fresh mushrooms and the onion until they are wilted and most of the pan liquid has evaporated.

Drain the porcinis. Save 1/4 cup of the liquid and pour through a very fine strainer. Reserve.
Rinse the porcinis well to remove sand, squeeze out excess water, chop them finely and add to the pan. Toss in the chopped sage and cook for 2 more minutes. Remove from the heat.

In a separate bowl beat the eggs with the cream and salt and the reserved porcini liquid.

Scatter the mushroom/onion mixture over the bottom of the pre-baked tart shell. Sprinkle the goat cheese over that and pour the custard over the top. Bake in a preheated 350° oven until the filling is set and slightly puffy. Let the tart set for 5 to 10 minutes before removing the tart from the pan and cutting into wedges.

K.T.

FOR THE DOUGH

1 cup warm water

1 tablespoon active dry yeast

1/2 teaspoon salt

2 cups semolina flour (available in some supermarkets and nutrition centers)

1 to 1 1/2 cups all purpose unbleached flour

1/4 cup olive oil

FOR THE FILLING

Olive oil for cooking eggs

5 large eggs

2 bunches fresh spinach, or two packages frozen

2 tablespoons olive oil

2 cloves garlic, minced

1 medium onion, minced

1 pound whole-milk ricotta cheese

1/2 cup sliced black olives

1 sweet red pepper, cut in 1/2x2-inch julienne

1/2 teaspoon dried oregano

1/2 teaspoon dried basil (or lots of fresh, chopped)

1 cup freshly grated parmesan cheese

1/2 pound grated mozzarella, provolone or fontina cheese

1/2 pound prosciutto or ham, diced

2 ounces sun-dried tomatoes, diced

TORTA RUSTICA

To make the dough, mix the yeast in the warm water. If you are working with a food processor, place the salt, semolina and one cup of the unbleached flour in the workbowl fitted with the dough blade. When the yeast is dissolved add the olive oil to the water and slowly pour into the machine while it is running. Allow a dough ball to form, adding more of the flour if the dough sticks to the sides of the workbowl. Allow the dough ball to rotate (knead) in the machine for 60 seconds after it forms.

If you are working with a mixer, place the water, dissolved yeast, olive oil and salt in the bowl. Attach the pastry paddle, then add half the flour while the machine is running to form a batter. Remove the paddle, attach the dough hook and add the remaining flour until a dough ball forms. Continue kneading for 6 to 8 minutes. The dough should be slightly sticky.

Place the dough in a gallon-size plastic bag; squeeze all the air out and place a wire twist at the *top* of the bag so the dough has room to expand. Allow to rise until it has doubled in size--about 1 hour--or overnight in the refrigerator. Preheat the oven to 425°. Grease a deep 9- or 10-inch pie plate with oil.

Beat two of the eggs together. Heat a small, heavy skillet over medium heat. Add 1 tablespoon of olive oil and, when it is hot, add the eggs and cook as for an omelette, just until the eggs are not runny anymore. Slip out onto a plate. Repeat with two more eggs. Set the egg layers aside.

Wash the fresh spinach and cook it with only the water that clings to the leaves, until it is just wilted. Drain, cool and squeeze out the remaining moisture in a clean towel. If you are using frozen spinach thaw it and squeeze out the moisture as above. Whichever spinach you are using, chop coarsely and reserve.

Heat 2 tablespoons of olive oil in a medium skillet over moderate heat. Add the garlic and onion, and sauté gently until they are soft but not browned. Place them in a large bowl and add the remaining egg, the chopped spinach, ricotta, olives, pepper, and seasonings. Stir to blend well.

On a floured surface roll out 2/3 of the dough to form a circle slightly larger than the pie plate. Gently fit the dough into the pan without stretching it, letting the sides overhang for the moment. Assemble the torta by placing one of the egg layers in the bottom; add half of the spinach-ricotta mixture, half of the grated parmesan and mozzarella, half of the diced prosciutto or ham and sun-dried tomatoes. Repeat with the remaining ingredients.

Roll out the remaining dough into a circle. Wet the edges of the bottom crust lightly, set the top crust in place and crimp the edges together decoratively. Cut several steam vents in the top. Brush with beaten egg for a shiny crust, if you like. Place the Torta in the preheated oven for 35 to 40 minutes. Allow to stand at least 15 minutes before cutting and serving. It seems equally good at room temperature or gently reheated the following day. Makes 8 to 12 servings.

This is one of my favorite breakfast or tea breads. This recipe makes 2 loaves. I use black baker's steel pans (9x5-inch loaf pans) to achieve a beautiful browning on all sides of the bread. This bread freezes very well, so make it ahead and thaw it the night before your lazy Sunday Brunch.

3 1/2 cups all purpose flour

1/2 teaspoon baking soda

4 teaspoons baking powder

1 teaspoon kosher salt

1/8 teaspoon freshly grated nutmeg

1/2 teaspoon cinnamon

2/3 cup butter, room temperature

1 1/3 cups sugar

4 large eggs, room temperature

2 cups mashed bananas (about 4 fully ripened bananas, easily done in a food processor)

3/4 cup chopped walnuts

1 cup diced dried apricots (tossed with a little flour to separate)

1/3 cup minced crystallized ginger (available in the Chinese section of a grocery store)

APRICOT-BANANA-GINGER BREAD

Preheat the oven to 350º.

Sift together the first six ingredients and set aside.

In the large bowl of an electric mixer cream the butter and sugar. Add the eggs, one at a time, and mix until smooth. Beat in the mashed bananas.

With the mixer on low, add the sifted ingredients in three batches to the banana mixture. Beat well after each addition.

Fold in the walnuts, apricots, and ginger. Blend well.

Divide the batter between 2 greased bread pans. Bake for 45 minutes or until a cake tester comes away clean when poked into the center of the bread. Cool for 10 minutes. Remove from the pans to a cooling rack and let cool completely before wrapping.

NOTE: I use a spray-on corn oil to grease my pans. For me, this has proven to be the most reliable method to keep my breads, muffins and other baked goods from sticking to the pans.

DM

Salmon Rillettes
Cold Grilled Lamb Salad
Lemon-Garlic Mayonnaise
Rye Bread
Spaghetti Squash Salad with Prosciutto
Pearl Onion Relish
Individual Huckleberry Tarts

———————————◆———————————

AN ELEGANT AUTUMN PICNIC

Beautiful, glorious, crisp Fall!! How I love this time of year! My only sadness comes from the fact that the end of picnic season is drawing near. Happily, there is usually time (and warmth!) for one final, elegant outdoor meal among the brilliant reds and glamorous golds of nature. So bring along a wonderful homemade and hearty bread. Use some of it to accompany a ravishing Rillettes of Salmon, but save enough to make sandwiches from some of the leftover cold, rare lamb a day or so later. Compose a Grilled Lamb Salad at the picnic table; it is easy to arrange and is perfect paired with Audrey's Lemon-Garlic Mayonnaise. Spaghetti Squash Salad with Prosciutto is an easy but very tasty addition to our menu. Diane suggests her Huckleberry Tarts, a truly memorable dessert made just as well with frozen blueberries or blackberries if you are suddenly short on wild huckleberries! We suggest starting the meal with a great Chardonnay or rich Chenin Blanc and continuing with a fine, full red wine--a Zinfandel or Pinot Noir, perhaps. This meal is really mouthwateringly elegant. I can't wait for an appropriately warm and colorful day in the fall!

Kathleen Taggart

SALMON RILLETTES

This recipe is from Lucien Vanel, owner of the restaurant Vanel in the old city of Toulouse in France. It first appeared in Cuisine Magazine in 1981 and has been a favorite of mine ever since. The rillette improves with age. It will keep up to 1 week under a layer of clarified butter. Plan to make it 2 days before serving since the flavors improve.

1 pound skinless fresh salmon filet, cut in 4 pieces

1/4 teaspoon kosher salt

9 tablespoons unsalted butter, divided, at room temperature

1 large shallot, minced

1/4 pound smoked salmon (lox), cut in 1/4-inch dice

1 tablespoon dry white wine

2 tablespoons olive oil

1 tablespoon lemon juice

1 egg yolk

Freshly ground pepper (preferably white), to taste

Pinch freshly grated nutmeg

Clarified butter for sealing

Sprinkle the salmon with the salt and let it stand at room temperature for 20 minutes.

In a small skillet or sauté pan heat 2 tablespoons of the butter until it foams. Add the shallots and sauté until soft but not browned. Add the salmon pieces and wine in one layer; cover with a piece of wax paper, then with a tight fitting lid, and let cook over medium heat for 2 minutes. Turn the salmon, cover again, and cook another 2 minutes or until just opaque. Remove the pan from the heat but leave it covered and cool the salmon in the pan. When the salmon is cool, flake it into the wine-shallot mixture, removing any bones which might appear.

In a food processor fitted with the metal blade, process the remaining 7 tablespoons of butter until it is creamy. Add the flaked salmon and the smoked salmon and pulse the machine until they are combined; the texture should be grainy--do not process until smooth. Add the olive oil, lemon juice, egg yolk and seasoning and pulse until combined. Taste and adjust seasonings.

Pack rillettes into either 2 1-cup crocks or 1 2-cup dish. Smooth the surface and pour melted clarified butter over the surface to cover by about 1/3 inch. Refrigerate uncovered.

To serve, remove the layer of butter by running a small, sharp knife around the rim of the dish and lifting off the butter. You may save it and use it for later cooking. Serve the rillettes at room temperature accompanied by bread or crackers.

NOTE: Clarified butter is butter which has been melted and the solids skimmed off, the butterfat carefully strained, leaving the milky residue to discard. It is a solid cooking fat when chilled and has no milky residue which burns in the pan. You may skip this step and just cover the crocks with plastic wrap if you are serving the rillettes within 2 days.

DM

1 5-pound leg of lamb, boned and butterflied

1/4 cup fresh lemon juice

1/4 cup olive oil

3 cloves garlic, minced

1/2 teaspoon dried thyme, or 1 1/2 teaspoons fresh

1 teaspoon dried rosemary or 1 tablespoon fresh

1 bay leaf, crumbled

2 tablespoons chopped parsley

1/2 teaspoon freshly ground black pepper

1/2 teaspoon salt

1 bunch fresh spinach or red leaf lettuce, washed and dried

1/2 cup Kalamata olives

3 plum tomatoes, cut in 4 to 6 wedges each

2 to 3 tablespoons toasted pine nuts

1 sweet red pepper, julienned

A few sprigs fresh mint, for garnish

COLD GRILLED LAMB SALAD

Trim the lamb of excess fat and remove the fell (thin membrane covering the meat). Divide the meat into two basic pieces, one thick and the other thinner, for easier grilling.

Combine the remaining ingredients for the marinade. Place the meat in a dish large enough to hold it in a single layer and cover with the marinade. Cover and refrigerate from anywhere between 3 and 24 hours.

Prepare the grill. When coals are white hot, sear the meat for 2 minutes on each side, at about 3 inches above the coals. Raise the grill to about 5 inches above the coals and continue cooking until the internal temperature of the meat reaches 135 to 140°, probably about 20 minutes.

Remove pieces as done and chill. This may be done several days before serving the salad.

To serve, carve the meat into thin slices across the grain and arrange as much of it as you wish on a large platter over the spinach or red leaf lettuce. Arrange the olives, tomatoes, pine nuts, red pepper and mint sprigs around the platter to present an attractive salad. Serve with the Lemon-Garlic Mayonnaise.

1 whole egg
2 egg yolks
1/2 cup fresh lemon juice, divided
1/2 teaspoon salt
1/2 teaspoon freshly ground black pepper
3 cloves garlic, peeled
2 1/4 cups good quality olive oil
1/2 teaspoon dried rosemary or 1 1/2 teaspoons fresh or 3 sprigs fresh mint, chopped (do not use dried mint!)

LEMON-GARLIC MAYONNAISE

In the bowl of a food procesor fitted with the metal blade place the egg, egg yolks, 1/4 cup of the lemon juice and salt and pepper. Process 1 minute. Add garlic cloves while the machine is running. Gradually add the olive oil in a thin stream until all of it has been incorporated into the other ingredients and an emulsion has formed. Taste for seasonings. You will probably want to add some or all of the remaining lemon juice. Add the rosemary or mint and process briefly to combine. Taste again. Transfer to an airtight container and refrigerate until ready to use.

Here is a rather simple rye loaf which goes well with the Rillettes of Salmon and Cold Grilled Lamb Salad, and is worth having around for general sandwich making, as well.

For 1 9x5-loaf pan:

1/4 cup warm milk
3/4 cup warm water
2 tablespoons molasses
1 tablespoon active dry yeast
2 1/4 cups all purpose unbleached flour, approximately
1 cup medium rye flour
1 teaspoon kosher salt
1/2 teaspoon caraway seeds
1 egg white, for glaze

RYE BREAD

Mix together the milk, water, molasses and yeast. Allow to become foamy. (Be careful to keep the liquid temperatures at 115º or below.)

If you are using a food processor mix the dough in the following manner: place all the dry ingredients in the workbowl fitted with the dough blade, if your machine has one. Stir the yeast mixture and slowly pour it into the workbowl while the machine is running. If you hear "sloshing" you are pouring too fast! Have some extra flour on the counter just in case your dough is too sticky and will not rotate inside the machine. When the dough ball has formed and is rotating, allow it to knead for 45 to 60 seconds.

If you are using a mixer, place the liquids in the bowl and fit the machine with the pastry paddle to speed the dough formation. Add about 1/2 the total flour and run on slow speed to obtain a batter-like consistency. Now remove the paddle and fit the dough hook and continue adding flour until the dough ball forms. Continue kneading for about 6 to 8 more minutes. The dough should clean the sides of the bowl.

Place the dough in a gallon-size plastic bag, squeeze out all of the air and place a wire twist at the *top* of the bag so that the dough has room to expand in the bag. Allow to approximately double in size, then remove from the bag, shape into a loaf to fit the pan, or make any free-form shape you like and place on a baking sheet. Allow to rise again until double its original size.

Preheat the oven to 375º. When ready to bake, brush the top of the loaf with the beaten egg white. Bake until golden brown and about 180º in the middle of the loaf--about 35 to 45 minutes. Cool on a rack before wrapping.

To serve 6:

1 large spaghetti squash, five pounds or more

2 ounces prosciutto, sliced thin, then julienned finely

4 scallions, cleaned and trimmed, white part and about 2 inches of green, thinly sliced

4 sprigs fresh thyme leaves (you may use dried, but fresh is better) stripped off the stems

1/4 cup extra virgin olive oil

1/4 cup plain salad oil--corn, safflower, soybean, peanut, etc.

3 tablespoons Balsamic red wine vinegar (a dark, very mellow wine vinegar available in specialty stores and some good supermarkets)

1/2 teaspoon dijon mustard

Pinch of kosher salt

Freshly ground black pepper, to taste

1/4 teaspoon sugar--optional

Cherry tomatoes and lettuce leaves, as garnish

SPAGHETTI SQUASH SALAD WITH PROSCIUTTO

Spaghetti squash is a wonderful and unusual vegetable that truly does shred into spaghetti-like strands when it is cooked. Several years ago we had invited some neighbors to dinner and were baking a large spaghetti squash in the oven--the whole, unsplit squash! While we were in the living room enjoying drinks and hors d'oeuvres a muffled boom was heard from the direction of the kitchen. Upon investigation we discovered strands of squash hanging from each oven rack and decorating the sides and bottom, too! Our neighbor (our favorite crazy artist) was sure the whole event had been orchestrated just for him and his wife and was pleased to eat the salvaged results, which were tossed with butter. So we encourage you to split the squash before baking it for this recipe!

Preheat the oven to 350º. Split the squash and clean out the seeds. Place open side down on a baking pan which has enough water in it to cover the bottom of the pan. Bake for about 1 hour, or until tender when pierced with a fork. Cool.

Scrape the flesh out into a bowl using a fork so that the strands separate. Toss in the prosciutto, scallions and thyme. Mix all the dressing ingredients and add to the salad. Do this a few hours before serving for best flavor.

Serve over lettuce pieces garnished with cherry tomatoes, either on one large platter or on individual plates.

K. T.

For 6 to 8 servings:

2 cups water

1 1/2 cups dry red wine

1/2 cup red wine vinegar

1/8 teaspoon cayenne pepper

1/4 teaspoon dried oregano

1/4 teaspoon dried thyme, or 4 or 5 sprigs fresh

1 cup sugar

1/2 cup olive oil

1 1/2 teaspoons kosher salt

Freshly ground black pepper

3 tablespoons vegetable oil

3 pounds frozen pearl onions

1 pound fresh green beans, cut into 1-inch pieces

2 small or 1 medium tomato, Roma if possible, peeled and diced about 1/4 inch

1/2 pound fresh mushrooms, small if possible, quartered

1 cup currants

1 cup minced fresh parsley

PEARL ONION RELISH

Here is a sweet-sour relish or salad or chutney, as you wish. I believe it to be perfect picnic fare in that it has forceful enough flavors to battle outdoor breezes and will benefit from having been made up several days in advance. The inspiration to develop this recipe was provided by Bert Greene's "Onions Beaulieu" in his excellent book KITCHEN BOUQUETS.

Place the water, wine, vinegar, cayenne, oregano, thyme, sugar, oil, salt and pepper in a saucepan or dutch oven of at least 5-quart capacity. Bring to a boil and simmer while you brown the onions.

In a large, heavy-bottomed skillet place the vegetable oil and heat until the oil "ripples." Add 1 pound of the onions and cook, stirring, until the onions brown somewhat. Adding a pinch of sugar during the cooking will help markedly in getting the onions to brown. Keep the heat at medium high or so. When the onions have browned remove them to a bowl and brown the second pound, then the third.

Add the browned onions to the liquid and cook for 10 minutes, uncovered. Add the green beans and cook, uncovered, until they are a bit tender. Add the tomatoes, mushrooms and currants and cook until they are softened. If the dish is still quite liquid, keep cooking to evaporate moisture; otherwise remove from the heat, taste for seasonings and chill. Mix in the parsley after the onions have cooled.

Best served at room temperature or just slightly cooled.

This makes 6 individual 4-inch tarts.
Use removable-bottom tart pans.

CRUST

2 cups unsifted all purpose flour

1/3 cup granulated sugar

1/8 teaspoon salt

1 1/2 sticks (6 ounces) unsalted butter, very cold or frozen, cut into tablespoon size pieces

1 large egg

1 teaspoon vanilla

FILLING

4 cups huckleberries (or use blackberries)

1/2 cup sugar

2 tablespoons tapioca

1/4 teaspoon almond extract

1/8 teaspoon salt

2 teaspoons orange flower water (available at specialty markets)

GLAZE

1 egg white

1 1/2 teaspoons orange flower water

INDIVIDUAL HUCKLEBERRY TARTS

To make the crust place the flour, sugar and salt in the workbowl of a food processor fitted with the metal blade. Pulse 2 or 3 times to combine. Add the very cold or frozen butter and pulse until the mixture resembles coarse bread crumbs.

Combine the egg and vanilla in a small measuring cup. You should have almost 1/3 cup. With the processor running, pour the liquids through the feed tube and process until the dough just hints at coming together. If the dough seems too dry add 1 tablespoon of ice water at a time until the dough just comes together around the blade.

Shape the dough into a 6-inch disk and wrap in plastic. Refrigerate for 1 hour before using. The dough can be frozen, tightly wrapped, and thawed for 1 hour at room temperature before rolling.

Make the filling while the dough is refrigerating. In a medium-sized bowl toss the berries with the sugar and tapioca. Add the almond extract, salt and orange flower water and stir gently to combine. Set aside for 1 hour, stirring occasionally to dissolve the sugar and tapioca.

Combine the egg white and orange flower water for the glaze and set aside.

Roll the dough into a large circle that is 1/8-inch thick. Using a small pot lid or thin rimmed bowl about 6 inches in diameter, cut circles of dough. Fit the dough into the tart pans and, using a rolling pin across the top of the tart pans, trim the excess dough from the pan. You should have 6 tart shells; if necessary reroll the dough trimmings to get the sixth shell. Refrigerate the shells for 20 minutes and preheat the oven to 450º.

Prick the bottom of the tarts all over with a fork. Brush all of the dough with the glaze. Divide the filling among the six tart pans and bake in the *lower third* of the oven for 15 minutes. Reduce the heat to 350º and continue baking for 20 minutes or until the crusts are nicely browned. Remove the tarts to a cooling rack and leave in the pans until ready to serve.

DM

Moussaka with Cheeses
Salad Vinaigrette with Wild Mushrooms
Whole Wheat Dill Braid
Bosc Pears Poached with White Wine and Ginger
Orange Custard Sauce

DINNER FOR GOOD FRIENDS

It seems that everywhere we turn today--magazines, newspapers, television, we find news stories admonishing us that our American diet is composed of too much meat. Vegetarianism has become increasingly popular among many of us, but for the majority it is not readily acceptable. We try, instead, to cut back on red meats and eat more poultry and fish. We usually associate meatless meals with things like beans, rice, lentils and other legumes and serve them occasionally, but not often.

Have I got news for you! Herewith we offer you a meatless menu that is elegant and delicious enough to serve to friends at dinner. It is definitely not dull or boring. The main course is Moussaka, my improvisation on the traditional Greek dish made with eggplant, potatoes, tomatoes and a cheese-herb-egg mixture topped with bechamel sauce and baked in the oven. If you really cannot stand eggplant then substitute zucchini squash, but my advice is to try my eggplant version first, or try half eggplant and half zucchini. To accompany the casserole we feature a delicate Salad Vinaigrette with Wild Mushrooms (more and more frequently available in supermarkets at certain times of the year) and a hearty Whole Wheat-Dill Braid. Finish the meal with Audrey's Bosc Pears Poached in White Wine and Ginger, which she likes to serve with an Orange Custard Sauce laced with Grand Marnier. It is a fitting end to this festive meal!!

Georgia M. Vareldzis

TOMATO SAUCE

1/2 cup olive oil

1 clove garlic, peeled

2 leeks, white part only, cleaned and chopped finely

1 rib celery chopped finely

1 28-ounce can tomatoes, drained and chopped, juice reserved

3 tablespoons tomato paste

1/4 cup dry red wine

1/2 cinnamon stick

2 bay leaves

1/2 teaspoon allspice

Salt and pepper, to taste

VEGETABLES

2 medium eggplants (about 1/2 to 3/4 pounds each) or 6 fairly large zucchini squash

6 large red potatoes

CHEESE FILLING

1 pound ricotta cheese

1/2 pound feta cheese

2 eggs

3 tablespoons chopped fresh dill, or 2 teaspoons dried

1/2 cup chopped fresh parsley

MOUSSAKA WITH CHEESES

This dish takes some effort to put together, but it can be prepared ahead, baked until about three quarters done, then cooled and refrigerated. It should be reheated before serving. For 6 to 8 persons.

Heat 1/4 cup of the olive oil in a large saucepan. Crush the clove of garlic into the oil. Add the leeks and celery, cooking over medium heat until the vegetables are soft but not browned--about 10 minutes. Add the tomatoes and reserved juice, tomato paste, wine, cinnamon stick and bay leaves. Bring to a boil, reduce to a simmer and cook until the sauce is quite thick and the liquid has nearly cooked away. Add the allspice. Taste for salt and pepper. This may be prepared a day ahead of time.

Cut the unpeeled eggplant and unpeeled potatoes lengthwise into 1/4-inch thick slices and place in a bowl of salted ice water for about 30 minutes. If you use zucchini do the same. Remove the vegetables from the water and dry well on paper towels. Line a large baking pan with foil and arrange the eggplant and potatoes in a single layer. Brush with the remaining 1/4 cup of olive oil, covering well. Brown under a preheated broiler on both sides. Use as large a pan as you have in order to reduce browning time. Set the vegetables aside and adjust the oven heat to 350°.

Combine the ricotta, feta cheese and eggs, and blend well. Stir in the herbs. Set aside.

Prepare the bechamel sauce by heating the butter in a medium-sized saucepan until the butter melts. Stir in the flour and cook gently for two or three minutes; this length of time is required to eliminate the raw flour taste. Add the milk, stirring constantly over medium heat until the sauce begins to thicken. This will happen more quickly if you have brought the milk to a simmer first. Remove from the heat. In a medium-sized bowl, beat the eggs slightly, then stir into them a cup or two of the hot milk mixture. Stir the egg mixture back into the sauce, along with the parmesan cheese. Taste for salt and pepper.

With the oil remaining on your brush from the eggplant and potatoes, brush the bottom of a 9x13-inch baking dish, such as a Le Creuset roaster. Layer half the eggplant and potatoes, cover with half the tomato sauce and all of the cheese filling. Layer in the remaining vegetables and tomato sauce. Cover with the bechamel sauce, spreading it evenly across the casserole.

BECHAMEL SAUCE

6 tablespoons butter

6 tablespoons flour

1 quart whole milk

2 eggs

1/2 cup grated parmesan cheese

Salt and pepper, to taste

To serve 6:

1/2 teaspoon dijon mustard

1/4 teaspoon kosher salt, to start

1/2 teaspoon sugar, to start

Freshly ground black pepper, to taste

2 tablespoons rice wine vinegar

6 tablespoons olive oil

2 tablespoons freshly minced parsley

1 tablespoon olive oil

1/2 pound wild mushrooms,
chanterelles, oyster mushrooms or
morels, sliced

1 large head of red leaf lettuce,
cleaned and dried

Bake in a preheated 350º oven until well-browned on top, about 1 to 1 1/4 hours. If you are making it ahead, bake for only 50 minutes, remove and cool the casserole; then reheat at 325º for 30 to 40 minutes. In either case, allow the moussaka to rest after baking--30 to 45 minutes if freshly baked, 20 minutes or so if reheating.

SALAD VINAIGRETTE WITH WILD MUSHROOMS

In a salad bowl mix the mustard, salt, sugar and pepper to form a paste. Add the rice vinegar and 6 tablespoons of olive oil and stir well to combine. Add the freshly minced parsley. Mix well and taste. Adjust the seasonings with more sugar and salt if needed. Taste again and keep adjusting if necessary. Set your salad servers over this mixture and lay the salad greens over the top.

Heat a heavy-bottomed sauté pan over high heat and add the olive oil. When the oil is hot, add the sliced mushrooms and stir constantly until they are lightly cooked. They should not be cooked so long that they give up their liquid. Set aside.

When ready to serve the salad, add the mushrooms to the salad bowl and toss. Serve on lightly chilled salad plates.

1/2 cup warm water

1/2 cup honey

1 tablespoon or package active dry yeast

3 large eggs at room temperature

3 cups all purpose unbleached flour, approximately

2 cups whole wheat flour

2 teaspoons kosher salt

1 stick (4 ounces) unsalted butter at room temperature

1 whole egg beaten, for glaze

WHOLE WHEAT DILL BRAID

In a small bowl or glass measure, mix the water and honey. This mixture should not be over 115º. Use an instant read thermometer to measure temperature if you are not sure. Stir in the yeast and allow to rest until this mixture is foamy, indicating that the yeast is alive. Stir in the eggs, beating enough to thoroughly blend everything.

If you are using a food processor mix the dough in the following manner: place all the dry ingredients in the workbowl fitted with the dough blade if the machine has one. (This recipe is too large for standard-size processors. It requires a machine with a flour capacity of at least 6 cups of flour; an 8-cup-size machine is better yet, as this is a fairly heavy dough.) Add the butter (cut into tablespoon-size pieces) to the workbowl and run the machine for 30 seconds or so in order to mix in the butter. Have an extra cup of flour on the counter in case you need "insurance" against a sticky dough. With the machine running, pour the liquids through the feed tube so that the flour absorbs the liquids, but not so fast that you hear "sloshing" in the bottom. In a minute or so a dough ball should begin to form, then look uniformly moist and begin to rotate around the workbowl. Continue this kneading for 45 seconds, adding flour if the dough seems too sticky to rotate, or water if the dough is dry and crumbly.

If you are using a mixer, place the liquids in the bowl and fit the machine with the pastry paddle to speed the dough formation. Add the salt and about half the total flour and run on slow speed to obtain a batter-like consistency. Add the butter and mix well to incorporate the butter. Now remove the paddle and fit the dough hook and continue adding flour until the dough ball forms. Continue kneading for about 6 to 8 more minutes. The dough should clean the sides of the bowl.

Place the dough in a gallon-size plastic bag, squeeze out all the air and place a wire twist at the *top* of the bag so that the dough has room to expand in the bag. Allow to rise slowly for an hour or more; this is usually a slow riser as breads go. Remove the dough from the bag and cut it into three equal pieces. Roll out each piece into a rope about 18 inches long, being sure to make them look uniform, and not like a snake that has just had a large meal! Gather together three ends and squeeze them firmly together. Now braid the loaf toward the other end, gathering the end pieces together and crimping them firmly to prevent the loaf from "unraveling". Arrange neatly on a greased, or cornmeal-coated, or parchment-papered baking sheet and cover with oiled plastic wrap.

Allow the dough to rise until the loaf looks about half again as large as it started out to be. Preheat the oven to 375º for 15 minutes.

Brush the loaf with beaten whole egg and bake it in the middle level of the oven until nicely browned, about 35 to 45 minutes. Turn the oven down to 325º if the loaf seems to be browning too rapidly. Test the center of the bread for 180º if you have an instant read thermometer. Transfer to a cooling rack gently, since braided loaves break easily.

This freezes well as long as it is wrapped in an airtight manner.

To serve 6:

Rind and juice of 1 lemon

1 one-inch piece fresh ginger, peeled and sliced

2 cups white wine

1 cup water

1/2 cup sugar

1 cinnamon stick

6 whole cloves

Pinch of cayenne pepper

6 Bosc pears, almost ripe

BOSC PEARS POACHED WITH WHITE WINE AND GINGER

Combine all ingredients but the pears in a large stainless steel or enamel pot. Bring to a boil over medium heat and simmer 5 minutes.

Peel the pears with a potato peeler, leaving the stems on. Leaving the pears whole, pierce the bulbous end of each pear with your potato peeler and, using a circular motion, remove the core.

If your pot will not accommodate all six pears at once, let the remaining ones sit covered in water with the juice of a lemon added.

Poach the pears about eight minutes on one side, then turn and cook for an additional 5 to 8 minutes. Test for doneness with a cake tester or thin skewer. The pears should gently resist. Remove as done.

Reduce poaching liquid over high heat to 1 1/2 cups of liquid. Pour over the pears, cover and chill. Serve with the Orange Custard Sauce.

---

6 egg yolks

1/3 cup sugar

1 cup whipping cream

1/2 cup milk

3 tablespoons Grand Marnier

1/2 teaspoon grated orange zest

ORANGE CUSTARD SAUCE

In the top of a double boiler or in a heat-proof bowl (I like Pyrex for this), whisk together the egg yolks and sugar until thick.

Scald the cream and milk. Add slowly to the egg yolk and sugar mixture, whisking constantly.

Cook, whisking, over simmering water until the mixture is thick and will coat a spoon heavily (about 175°-180° on an instant read thermometer).

Remove from the heat. Strain into a clean bowl and whisk occasionally until cool. Add the Grand Marnier and orange zest. Chill well.

To serve, pour a small pool of custard sauce onto a dessert plate and place a poached pear in the center. Garnish with candied orange peel or candied ginger if desired.

Caponata
Fresh Fettuccine with Oysters
Watercress, Sweet Red Pepper, and Cucumber Salad
Apple Phyllo Tart

A FEAST
MADE WITH OYSTERS

ince the Pacific Northwest is blessed with some of the world's finest oysters what could be more appropriate than an autumn dinner celebrating that glorious bivalve! We begin with Caponata, a sweet-tart mixture of eggplant, onion and tomato designed to tantalize your taste buds! It can be made several days ahead and, indeed, should sit at least 24 hours before serving to ensure the optimum marriage of flavors. Our entreé is a rich blend of Fresh Fettuccine with Oysters bound together by a sauce made with reduced cream, flavored with bacon and shallots and a hint of tomato. The sauce may be prepared ahead of time and gently reheated while the water for the pasta comes to a boil. We have complemented this rich main dish with a light and peppery watercress salad. It is refreshing served after the oysters and pasta and provides a texture and flavor contrast. Finally, we commissioned Georgia to create a memorable dessert for our menu. She did. We ate some of it, and agreed...it is ethereal!

Audrey Urbanowicz

2 pounds fresh eggplant, peeled and cut in 1 inch cubes

1/2 cup olive oil

2 tablespoons pine nuts

2 cups thinly sliced celery, with leaves

1 or 2 thinly sliced red or yellow peppers, if in season

1 medium onion, halved and thinly sliced

2 cloves garlic, peeled and minced

1/3 to 1/2 cup red wine vinegar, to your taste

1 1/2 tablespoons sugar

1 large (28-ounce) can peeled tomatoes, drained

2 tablespoons tomato paste

6 large green or black Mediterranean olives, pitted and slivered

2 tablespoons capers

4 anchovy fillets, rinsed and mashed

Salt and pepper, to taste

CAPONATA

This appetizer is served cold with fresh bread or on an antipasto buffet. It makes about 8 cups or enough to serve about 10 to 12 persons.

Sprinkle the eggplant cubes with a little salt and set in a colander to drain for 1/2 hour. Rinse and pat dry.

Heat half the olive oil in a heavy-bottomed skillet and sauté the pine nuts until they are golden. Remove them and set aside. Add the celery--and the peppers, if using--and cook over moderate heat, stirring, for 10 minutes. Add the onion and garlic and cook until all ingredients are soft and translucent. Remove with a slotted spoon and place in a bowl.

Pour the remaining oil into the pan and add the eggplant. Sauté over high heat, stirring constantly, until lightly browned. This should take 8 to 10 minutes. Return the celery-onion mixture to the pan. Add the remaining ingredients except the salt and pepper (starting with the smaller amount of vinegar) and stir together. Taste and season to your liking with salt and pepper.

Bring to a boil, reduce to a simmer and cook uncovered for 15 to 20 minutes, stirring occasionally. Stir in the pine nuts. Taste again and adjust the seasonings, adding more vinegar if you feel the need, and salt or pepper. Transfer to a bowl and refrigerate until serving time.

To serve 6:

6 slices bacon

2 10-ounce jars fresh oysters, medium or extra small, drained (available in the refrigerator case of markets selling fresh fish)

2 tablespoons unsalted butter

2 tablespoons olive oil

4 large shallots, minced

2 cloves garlic, minced

1/2 cup dry vermouth

2 tablespoons tomato paste

1 teaspoon dried thyme

1/2 teaspoon freshly grated nutmeg

Salt and freshly ground black pepper, to taste

1/2 cup heavy cream

1 1/2 pounds fresh egg fettuccine

1/2 cup heavy cream

1/3 cup freshly grated parmesan cheese

Minced fresh parsley, for garnish

FRESH FETTUCCINE WITH OYSTERS

Cook the bacon until barely crisp; drain well and dice. Set aside. Slice oysters into halves or thirds.

In a large sauté pan heat the butter and olive oil over medium heat. Cook the shallot and garlic until soft but not browned. Raise the heat a little and add the oysters, cooking them for 1 to 2 minutes. Using a slotted spoon remove the oysters to a plate.

Blend the vermouth and tomato paste and add to the pan along with the seasonings. Let this come to a boil and cook briefly, reducing the liquid a bit. Add the cream, bring to a boil and cook, reducing the cream's volume so that it thickens slightly. Taste for seasonings and adjust, tasting again. Remove from the heat and set aside.

In an 8-quart or larger pot bring 6 quarts of water to a boil. Add a couple of pinches of salt and about 1 tablespoon of vegetable or olive oil. Add the pasta and cook 3 to 5 minutes. Taste a piece for doneness, draining when just cooked. There is no need to rinse the noodles unless you are preparing them ahead of time. In that case rinse them with cold water, drain well, and toss with just enough oil to prevent the pasta from sticking together. Cover and refrigerate.

Heat the cream in a skillet or pot large enough to accommodate the oysters, sauce and pasta. Let it boil and reduce by half. Add the sauce and heat through. Add the bacon, oysters and drained pasta, stirring, and cook until the pasta is well-coated with the sauce. Add 1/4 cup of the parmesan cheese, blend, and turn the mixture into a large, heated serving bowl. Garnish with the remaining cheese and the minced parsley.

1 1/2 heads Boston or butter lettuce, cleaned and dried

1 bunch watercress, tough stems removed and leaves picked over

1 large sweet red pepper, cored, then julienned into 1-inch lengths

1 pound English cucumber, sliced crosswise into 1/4-inch thick slices, then julienned

2 tablespoons freshly minced parsley

4 tablespoons freshly minced cilantro*

VINAIGRETTE

2 tablespoons rice wine vinegar

6 tablespoons olive oil

3/4 teaspoon kosher salt

1 teaspoon sugar

Freshly ground black pepper, to taste

WATERCRESS, SWEET RED PEPPER AND CUCUMBER SALAD

Stack the prepared lettuce leaves, roll to form a cigar shape, then cut crosswise to obtain 1/2-inch wide shreds. Reserve.

In a large salad bowl combine the lettuce, watercress, sweet red pepper, cucumber, parsley and cilantro. Toss lightly. Cover completely with a damp but not wet paper towel. Reserve until serving, but not more than 2 hours.

In a glass jar with a tight fitting lid combine the vinegar, oil, salt, sugar and pepper. Close the jar, shake well and taste. Add more sugar, salt or pepper to adjust the seasonings, then taste again. Reserve.

When ready to serve, toss the salad with the vinaigrette just until combined and serve on lightly chilled salad plates.

NOTE: All salad components can be prepared early on the day you plan to serve. Wrap each salad ingredient separately and keep refrigerated.

* If you are one of those persons to whom cilantro tastes like soap, then substitute either an equal amount of freshly minced basil or 2 more tablespoons of the freshly minced parsley.

DM

APPLE PHYLLO TART

Use a 10-inch tart pan or pie plate. Makes 8 to 10 servings.

Preheat the oven to 350°. Put the prepared apples in a large, heavy-bottomed pot with the sugars, spices and lemon juice. Heat to a boil and cook over moderately high heat until the apples become golden brown and tender. This will take between 10 and 20 minutes depending on how green the apples are. You need to stir and watch them carefully after the first 5 minutes or so. Do not overcook! You do not want to make chunky applesauce!

4 to 5 large cooking apples (I prefer Rome Beauty), peeled, cored and sliced 1/8 inch thick. You should have 10 to 12 cups of apple slices.

1 cup granulated sugar

1/2 cup brown sugar

1 teaspoon cinnamon

1/2 teaspoon nutmeg, freshly grated is best

2 tablespoons lemon juice

Zest of 1 lemon

2 tablespoons finely chopped pistachios, or other nuts

1 tablespoon Grand Marnier

1 stick (4 ounces) unsalted butter, melted

9 sheets phyllo (available in the frozen foods section at many better supermarkets)

1 tablespoon apricot preserves, heated

2 egg yolks

1/2 cup heavy cream

Drain the apples, reserving the syrup. Cool the apples slightly. If you put them on the phyllo while hot the dough will become soggy. Add the lemon zest, nuts and Grand Marnier to the apples in a bowl and toss to combine.

With a pastry brush, butter the phyllo sheets one at a time. Fold each sheet into thirds lengthwise, buttering each new surface as you fold it. Lay these strips over the bottom of the pan, with one end of the phyllo strip placed at the *base of the side* of the pan, and the excess dough allowed to hang over the opposite edge of the pan. Overlap the strips so that the entire bottom surface of the pan is covered.

Spread the preserves over the phyllo in the bottom of the pan. Spread the cooked apples evenly over the preserves.

Mix the egg yolks and cream well and pour over the apples.

Now fold each strip of phyllo toward the center of the pan, twisting it at the same time so as to form a sort of rosette. The dough will not cover the center of the tart. Most of the filling will probably show.

Place the tart pan on a baking sheet that has sides to catch any butter dripping out during the baking. Place the tart in your oven and bake until the phyllo is golden brown and the custard is set. Reduce the oven heat to 300º or 325º if it seems to be browning too quickly. Do not cover the dough! Baking time will be about 45 minutes to 1 hour.

Allow the tart to stand at least 30 minutes before cutting; serve warm or at room temperature, drizzling a little of the cooled syrup over the open custard if you like.

CHINESE MUSHROOM BROTH

This is an easy and light soup which makes a good accompaniment to a multi-dish meal. It requires precious little from the cook save the ability to make a decent meat stock. And, in a pinch, canned broth can be used with a slight drop in flavor quality. Serves 6 persons.

To make the stock, place the cut up chicken in a large saucepan or stockpot and cover with water. Bring to a boil, reduce to a simmer and skim off the brown foam which rises to the top for the next few minutes. When the foam becomes white rather than brown add the scallion, cut in two or three pieces, along with the ginger. Cover, reduce heat to maintain the barest simmer and cook for three to four hours. Strain the stock and remove the fat (a fat separator sold at kitchenware specialty stores makes this quite easy); or refrigerate the strained stock overnight and remove the congealed fat later.

To make the soup, have ready a tureen in which to serve the soup or the kitchen pan of your choice. It is nicest to take the tureen or pot to the table along with the rest of the meal so that the dinner guests may serve themselves as they wish during the dinner, but the soup can also be served as a first course after the springroll appetizers.

Heat the stock in a pan, adding the Chinese black mushrooms, soy sauce, sherry and sesame oil. Simmer gently for 5 minutes. Taste for seasonings, adding more of any of the seasonings you wish. *Do not* add any salt until you have adjusted the soy flavor to your liking first! Add the chili seasoning sparingly, if you are using it, and taste again. Thicken slightly if you desire by stirring together a cornstarch/water mixture (3 tablespoons of cornstarch mixed with 3 tablespoons of cold water) and drizzling it into the soup, stirring constantly. Pour the egg over the tines of a fork or just stir it in with a chopstick. Add the sliced scallion and fresh mushrooms and serve.

SPRINGROLLS

This recipe will make 20 to 25 lightly packed rolls, about twice what you will need for an appetizer for 6 persons. Freeze the extra cooked springrolls for later rewarming in a 350º oven. They are excellent for a quick lunch or dinner or as part of any meal you like.

The use of Lumpia (Philippine style) wrappers will produce a thin and crispy roll, more tender than the Chinese style eggroll wrappers. They are quite frayed around the edges and have a nasty tendency to stick together, but patience works and will be rewarded in the eating! Use the supermarket eggroll wrappers if you are short on patience. Lumpia wrappers are usually found in the freezer case of Oriental markets and are best defrosted overnight in the refrigerator. The ones not used may be tightly wrapped and refrozen or kept in the refrigerator for a week or two.

Combine the ginger, garlic and scallion in a small bowl or saucer. Reserve. Mix together the soy, sherry, wine vinegar, oyster sauce and sesame oil, and set aside. Have the cornstarch/water mixture ready, with a fork or chopstick handy for stirring.

1 walnut-size piece fresh ginger, unpeeled, minced

1 clove fresh garlic, minced

1 medium scallion, minced

1 tablespoon black soy sauce

1 tablespoon dry sherry

1 tablespoon rice wine vinegar

1 tablespoon oyster sauce

2 teaspoons dark-colored sesame oil

About 3 tablespoons cornstarch mixed with 3 tablespoons cold water

1/2 pound ground pork

3 to 5 tablespoons peanut or corn oil, for stir-frying

4 cups thinly shredded Napa cabbage

1 medium carrot, finely shredded

4 dried Chinese black mushrooms, softened in hot water, stems trimmed and discarded, minced

2 ounces cellophane noodles (bean threads, Chinese vermicelli, etc.) or a bunch about the size of a small zucchini, soaked until tender, drained and cut into 1/2-inch lengths

1 package Lumpia wrappers or other similar sized wrappers

2 eggs, lightly beaten

6 to 8 cups peanut or corn oil for deep frying

Using a chef's knife, Chinese cleaver or food processor, chop the ground pork a little finer without making it into a paste.

Heat a wok or large, heavy skillet until hot, then add 1 to 2 tablespoons of oil, swirling it around to coat the pan. Add the pork and stir fry, breaking up any large bits, until it is mostly grey in color. Remove from the wok, drain and reserve. While the wok is still hot rinse it out with hot water and dry with a paper towel.

Heat the wok again and add 2 to 3 tablespoons of oil until it is hot but not smoking. Add the garlic, ginger and scallion mixture, stir frying without burning for 30 seconds. Toss in the cabbage and carrot over high heat and stir fry a minute or two until the color of the vegetables brightens. Add the mushrooms, noodles, reserved pork mixture and the liquid seasonings and stir to mix.

When the liquids have come to a boil, stir the cornstarch mixture, pour a little of it into the pan, then stir while cooking to combine and thicken. The filling should be neither stiff nor runny, just a bit "sluggish." Add more thickening mixture if necessary. Remove the filling to a plate to cool until you can handle it. This may be done 2 or 3 days in advance if you like.

To make the rolls, separate the Lumpia wrappers gently and patiently, one at a time. Place a wrapper on a plate or countertop and brush egg all around the edge. Place about 2 rounded tablespoons of filling in the shape of a cigar about a third of the way up from the edge of the wrapper nearest you. Fold the bottom of the wrapper up and over the filling, brushing this new surface with egg as well. Fold the sides over to form two straight edges and roll up the springroll to enclose. Place the springrolls seam side down on a baking sheet while making the other rolls. These are best cooked within the hour, keeping them covered so as not to let them dry out.

To fry the rolls, heat the oil to 375° in a wok or large and deep saucepan or electric deepfryer. Do not have much beyond half the pan filled with oil so that the bubbles produced by the cooking cannot spill over the sides of the pan! Line a cookie sheet with three layers of paper towels for draining the rolls. Fry the rolls, four or five at a time, until they are nicely browned, about 2 to 3 minutes. Remove to drain, then serve immediately. They may be held briefly in a warm oven but will begin to lose crispness right away.

A good but simple sweet-sour sauce can be made as follows: mix equal parts of rice wine vinegar, light soy sauce and plum sauce or apricot jam, heating to dissolve the jam. Taste for sweetness, adding more vinegar and/or soy if the sauce is too sweet.

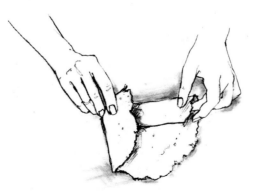

Ingredients

1 pound boneless chicken breast (or pork), trimmed of skin and fat, cut into 1-inch pieces

MARINADE

1/2 teaspoon salt

1 tablespoon dry sherry

1 egg white

1 tablespoon cornstarch

3 quarts water, for blanching the meat

1/4 cup chicken stock or water

1 tablespoon dark soy sauce

1 tablespoon light soy sauce

1 tablespoon Chinese black vinegar

1 tablespoon dry sherry

1 tablespoon sugar

2 teaspoons dark-colored sesame oil

1 1/2 tablespoons Chinese salted black beans, rinsed and coarsely chopped

3 tablespoons cornstarch mixed with 3 tablespoons water

1/2 cup raw cashews, toasted

6 dried red chilies, whole, or 3/4 teaspoon crushed red chilies

2 cloves garlic, minced

2 quarter-size slices ginger, minced

3 medium scallions, cut diagonally into 1/2-inch pieces

1 sweet red pepper, cut into 1/2-inch pieces

4 to 6 tablespoons oil, for stir frying

SPICY CHICKEN OR PORK WITH CASHEWS

Sometimes in a stir fry the meat or seafood is partially cooked a bit in advance to make a better textured dish; coincidentally, it also gives the cook a chance to get some preparation out of the way early! Such is the case here. The chicken or pork could well be precooked 2 or 3 days in advance. If you plan to serve this dish separate from the menu, then I suggest serving it with at least two other dishes, such as steamed rice or simple noodles and a vegetable dish (which could be done days in advance and served at room temperature).

Stir the marinade ingredients together and toss with the chicken. Cover and refrigerate if holding more than an hour. Allow to marinate at least 30 minutes.

Bring the water to a boil and stir in the chicken. Blanch just until its surface turns mostly white, about 45 to 60 seconds. Drain immediately--this is only a partial cooking. This may be done 2 or 3 days in advance.

Before stir frying mix together the stock, soy sauces, vinegar, sherry, sugar, sesame oil, and black beans. Have a fork or chopstick ready to stir the cornstarch mixture. If the cashews are raw, toast them under a broiler.

Heat a wok or large, heavy skillet until hot. Swirl in 3 to 4 tablespoons of the oil. If you are using the *whole chilies* add them now, keeping the heat at medium so they will not burn. They should turn nearly black in a minute or two but not burn immediately!

Add the garlic and ginger, raising the heat a bit, and stir fry about 30 seconds to release their flavors. If you are using the *crushed chilies* add them to the pan now and stir fry another 15 seconds or so.

Raise the heat to high and add the scallions and pepper, stir frying them a minute or two until their color brightens.

Add the liquid seasonings and the meat. As soon as the sauce boils, thicken it by adding a tablespoon or two of the cornstarch mixture and stirring, repeating until you have the texture of sauce that you like. Remove to a platter and serve, garnished with the nuts.

NOTE: If you use the whole dried chilies either remove them from the wok after their initial cooking *or* warn your guests not to eat them! I leave them in for garnish sake, but eating one is a guaranteed trip to the antacid bottle!

NOTE: Black beans are preserved with salt and ginger. Some have "five spice powder" added; do not use that type for this recipe or a licorice flavor will result. Read the label.

1 pound fresh egg noodles, any size, cooked, drained and refreshed under cold running water

2 tablespoons light soy sauce

1 tablespoon dark soy sauce

3 tablespoons rice vinegar or Chinese black vinegar

2 teaspoons sugar

1/4 cup peanut butter, softened

1 tablespoon dark-colored sesame oil

2 tablespoons vegetable oil

3 scallions, shredded

COLD TOSSED SESAME NOODLES

Here is a very easy dish which could be the backbone of a lunch or light dinner or, as in this case, part of a larger Chinese-style meal. In this menu it is served along with soup and a stir fry. It may be prepared several days ahead of time so as not to cause the cook worry at the last minute.

Prepare the noodles and set aside. Mix the next 7 ingredients and reserve.

Shred the scallions using a Chinese cleaver or chef's knife, working almost lengthwise on the scallions as if you were going to cut them into thin and very long strips. Precision is not necessary. Toss most of the scallions and the seasoning mixture with the noodles. Add the remaining scallions over the top as a garnish when serving.

Serve at room temperature, not ice cold. If the noodles have become a bit dry during refrigeration you may want to toss them with a little extra vegetable oil before serving.

This dessert relies on the natural sweetness of ripe pears for its appeal. If they are not in season good substitutes might include cantaloupe or honeydew melons or berries of nearly any kind. It is best made the same day you plan to serve it so as to avoid the formation of ice crystals; at most make it 3 to 4 days in advance.

1 pound ripe, fresh pears (Comice are best), peeled, cored and cut in 1-inch pieces

1 teaspoon finely chopped orange zest

About 1/4 to 1/2 cup heavy cream

FROZEN PEAR CREAM

Place the pear pieces on a cookie sheet or platter and put in the freezer overnight or for at least 5 hours. They must be quite frozen!

Fit the bowl of a food processor with the metal blade. Add the fruit and pulse (turning the machine on and off rapidly) until the chunks are smaller, then run the machine until the pears are a fine frozen powder. Add the orange zest and, with the machine running, slowly pour in the cream until the fruit begins to mass together and take on the look of soft ice cream. Scrape the workbowl down if necessary. Run the machine only until you like the texture of the dessert.

Serve immediately or freeze for later use.

Curried Shrimp over Spaghetti
Tapenade Fettuccine with Grilled Shark
Pepper and Almond Lasagne
Cucumber-Melon Salad
Insalata Composta
Frozen Kir Sherbet

PASTA BUFFET

ately pasta has taken on the role of "power food!" It is a true delight that something which tastes so good can be so good for you, too. We have incorporated this "power food" into a fun and unusual buffet which can serve 14 to 16 people very well. This is the type of entertaining I love--casual, relaxed and slightly unexpected!

Our buffet includes three unique pasta dishes. Dan's Curried Shrimp over Spaghetti has East Indian overtones which result from slightly exotic but easily found ingredients. I have created two dishes for this menu: a Tapenade Pasta with Grilled Shark and a Pepper and Almond Lasagne. The lasagne can be cooked in advance and reheated or put together in advance and cooked just before serving. Tapenade, a wonderful olive spread hinting of southwest France, can be prepared a couple of weeks in advance; you can also purchase one of several good imported versions!

To carry the menu's international flavor further Georgia suggests a delicious composed salad with Italian overtones while Audrey offers her refreshing Cucumber-Melon Salad with hints of East India again. Finally, Georgia's Frozen Kir Sorbet calls for a French-style Creme de Cassis liqueur made from black currants.

As always you can avoid last minute kitchen panic by making some foods ahead. The sorbet and tapenade could be made a week in advance; the Pepper and Almond Lasagne can be finished a day or two early and the two salads can happily be assembled a couple of hours before serving. The shrimp sauce may be reduced for thickening an hour or two early, so the real last minute chores are grilling the shark and finding a good friend to watch a couple of pots of boiling noodles!

Here's to good tastes!

Kathleen Taggart

This is a creamy dish which is quite easy to prepare but will leave you wishing for leftovers to reheat! It uses curry paste, a bottled product available in Oriental markets or some specialty food shops. If you cannot find curry paste--Daw Senn is a good brand--then you can stir 2 or 3 tablespoons of curry powder into the cream as it cooks and adjust the flavor from there.

2 cups heavy cream

2 large cloves garlic, thinly sliced

3 tablespoons butter

2 slices (about 1/2-inch) from a large onion, cut into large dice

3 to 4 medium scallions, sliced diagonally about 1/4-inch thick

2 small tomatoes (Roma variety is good) peeled, seeded and diced about 1/2-inch thick

1/4 cup peanut butter

1/4 cup curry paste

1/2 teaspoon garam masala (see note)

12 ounces salad shrimp (the tiny precooked kind)

7 or 8 ounces dried spaghetti

Minced parsley, scallion greens or chopped cilantro, as garnish

CURRIED SHRIMP OVER SPAGHETTI

Place the cream in a large saucepan over medium high heat. Add the garlic and boil down the cream by about 40 percent, so that it is a little over half its original volume. Adjust the heat so that it does not boil over the sides of the pan. It loves to make a mess of your range, so watch it closely!

In a 9- or 10-inch skillet cook the onion and scallion in the butter until it is limp but not brown. Add the onion and scallions to the cream mixture along with the tomatoes, peanut butter and curry paste. Stir in the garam masala and keep the sauce on low heat.

Bring 6 or 7 quarts of water to a boil in a large pot. Toss in 2 teaspoons of salt, then add the spaghetti and cook until it is just done--tender but not mushy! Drain well and toss with the sauce and the shrimp. Garnish, if you like, with a little chopped parsley, scallion greens or chopped fresh cilantro.

NOTE: Garam masala is a generic name for several different blends of Indian spices. Indian specialty stores stock it, or you can make your own:

2 teaspoons cardamom seeds (measured after removing from the pods)
1 teaspoon whole cloves
2 teaspoons grated nutmeg
3 cinnamon sticks
1 tablespoon coriander seeds

In a heavy-bottomed dry skillet cook the spices over medium heat, shaking the pan now and then, until they color slightly but do not burn. This may take from 1 to 4 minutes or so. Transfer the spices to a plate or bowl and, when cool, crush or grind them into a powder. Bottle and store for 6 months or so.

TAPENADE FETTUCCINE WITH GRILLED SHARK

1 1/2 pounds fish steaks cut about 1-inch thick--use shark, swordfish, marlin, tuna, etc.

2 tablespoons olive oil

2 tablespoons fresh lemon juice

A few crushed sprigs fresh sage, or a sprinkle of dried

1 large eggplant, thickly sliced, unpeeled

1 large onion, thickly sliced

Approximately 1/2 cup olive oil

1 pound fresh fettuccine noodles

6 ounces tapenade, homemade or good quality bottled

1/4 pound myzithra cheese, grated, or use romano

This is an earthy combination of flavor and texture. Tapenade is versatile and great to have around as a dip or spread! This dish involves several steps, but each is quick. If you have made the tapenade in advance the remaining work takes a little over half an hour! A large platter makes for a nice presentation.

Marinate the fish in the 2 tablespoons of olive oil, the lemon juice and the sage for 30 to 60 minutes before cooking.

Brush the eggplant and onion slices with the 1/2 cup or more of olive oil. Brown them on the grill of a well-heated barbecue; the eggplant will likely take 15 to 20 minutes to brown, depending on the heat. Then cut the cooked eggplant into 1/2 inch cubes. Separate the onion into rings.

Cook the fettuccine in a large pot of boiling, salted water until just done. Drain and toss with the tapenade and the eggplant cubes, the onion rings and 3/4 of the cheese. Keep warm on a serving platter while you grill the fish, about 5 minutes per side or about 10 minutes for each inch of thickness. Fish steaks or fillets on a grill are usually cooked and juicy, we find, when an instant read thermometer registers 120º to 125º. Above that temperature they tend to be a bit drier.

Place the fish in the center of a large platter, surrounded by the pasta. Sprinkle on the remaining cheese and serve immediately.

K. T.

PAULA WOLFERT'S TAPENADE DE TOULOUSE

1 2-ounce can anchovy fillets, packed in oil, drained

18 cured black olives, pitted, soaked overnight in olive oil with a few slivers of garlic

1 tablespoon dijon mustard

1 egg yolk

2/3 cup fruity olive oil

1 tablespoon fresh lemon juice

Cayenne pepper

This recipe is from Paula's wonderful book THE COOKING OF SOUTH-WEST FRANCE. It is my favorite version of this savory anchovy-oil dip.

Place the anchovies in a small bowl. Cover with water and let soak for 20 minutes. Drain.

Combine the anchovies, olives and mustard in the workbowl of a food processor fitted with the steel blade. Process until coarsely chopped.

Add the egg yolk and blend until smooth. With the machine running add the oil in a steady stream. Add lemon juice and season to taste with cayenne pepper. Spoon into a 1-cup crock. Makes about 3/4 cup.

PEPPER AND ALMOND LASAGNE

1 pound spinach lasagne noodles (egg noodles are fine, just not as colorful)

3 to 4 tablespoons olive oil

3 large sweet red peppers

3 large yellow peppers

1 teaspoon dried basil

2 large garlic cloves

1 pound whole-milk ricotta cheese

2 large eggs

3 tablespoons créme fraiche or heavy cream

4 dashes Tabasco sauce

1/2 bunch parsley leaves, washed and dried

Salt and freshly ground pepper, to taste

5 ounces grated Parmesan Reggiano, or other high quality grating cheese

4 ounces slivered, blanched almonds, toasted

Here is a marvelous meatless lasagne--very colorful and full of fresh goodies! You may use dry or fresh lasagne noodles. You will not need to cook the fresh variety--they will cook sufficiently while baking.

Cook the lasagne in lots of boiling salted water until just tender, but *not* mushy! Drain and toss in a bowl with the olive oil so the noodles do not stick together.

Steam or microwave both types of peppers until soft. Remove the stems and seeds. Purée each color separately, adding 1/2 teaspoon basil to each batch. Set aside.

In a food processor fitted with the metal blade mince the garlic. Add the ricotta, eggs, crème fraiche or heavy cream, Tabasco, parsley and salt and pepper to taste, and process until the mixture is smooth, scraping down the workbowl at least once.

Preheat the oven to 325º. Oil or butter a 9x13 baking pan. Place a layer of noodles on the bottom and cover with about 1/5 of the ricotta mixture. Top with half the yellow pepper purée and a tablespoon or so each of the grated cheese and almonds.

Top with another layer of noodles and layer as before, this time using the red pepper purée. Build another layer using yellow pepper purée, and another using red pepper purée. The final layer is made of noodles, the ricotta mixture and the last of the grated cheese.

Bake uncovered for about 35 minutes or until heated through. Let rest 10 to 15 minutes before cutting and serving.

Serves 6 to 8 as a main course, 12 or more as part of this buffet.

K. T.

CUCUMBER-MELON SALAD

1 English cucumber, cut in 1-1/2-inch chunks (if English cucumbers are not available use regular ones, peeled)

1/2 cantaloupe, peeled and cut in 1-1/2-inch chunks

1 tablespoon minced fresh mint

1 tablespoon minced fresh cilantro

1/2 cup plain yogurt

1 teaspoon ground cumin, toasted in an ungreased skillet over low heat for 30 seconds

Salt the cucumber chunks lightly and let them rest on paper towels for 30 minutes. Wipe off salt or rinse and dry well.

Combine all ingredients and refrigerate, covered, for at least 1 hour.

INSALATA COMPOSTA

3 waxy boiling potatoes (red-skinned or white Shastas, for example), cooked, cooled, and peeled

1 English cucumber, or 2 regular cucumbers, peeled such that narrow strips of peel remain

3 medium tomatoes, peeled

1/4 pound piece of Molinari or Genoa salami (or use any very firm, wine cured salami), white rind removed and sliced thinly but not paper thin

1/3 cup Mediterranean olives--black, green, purple or a mixture

6 tablespoons good quality olive oil

2 tablespoons freshly squeezed lemon juice

1 clove garlic, crushed (optional)

1 tablespoon chopped fresh basil or 1 teaspoon dried

Salt and freshly ground pepper, to taste

Lemon wedges

This is a composed, not a tossed salad. In a composed salad the ingredients are arranged in a pattern and served, rather than being mixed together.

Slice the potatoes, cucumbers and tomatoes about 1/4 inch thick. Arrange slices of salami, potato, cucumber and tomato in an alternating pattern on a large platter with a rim to catch the dressing. Put some olives around the edge, or in the center or in any pattern that suits you.

Mix the olive oil, lemon juice and garlic (if used). Chop the basil very finely and add to the dressing. Season with salt and pepper. Drizzle the dressing all over the salad. Serve with lemon wedges.

Note: Tomatoes are easily peeled by plunging them into boiling water for 10 to 15 seconds, rinsing under cold water and pulling the skin off with a paring knife.

FROZEN KIR SHERBET

Kir is an aperitif served in France. It is a combination of dry white wine and créme de cassis (a liqueur made from black currants).

1 cup dry white wine

3/4 cup sugar (if you use berries which have had sugar added then use only 1/2 cup sugar)

1 pint fresh raspberries, or 1 10-ounce package frozen, thawed

1/3 cup creme de cassis

2 cups half and half

In a small saucepan heat the wine and sugar to boiling. Cook for 5 minutes to make a syrup and cool.

Purée the berries in a food processor or blender. Sieve the purée to remove the seeds. Mix it with the syrup and liqueur and refrigerate until very cold--preferably overnight.

Stir in the half and half and freeze the mixture according to the instructions for the machine you are using. If you do not have an ice cream maker but do have a food processor then do the following: pour the mixture into a loaf pan or ice cube tray without dividers and freeze until almost firm--about 1 to 3 hours. Break into chunks and place it in a food processor fitted with the metal blade. Run the machine until the mixture is fluffy, but not until is has thawed completely. Serve at once or refreeze until serving time.

Scallion-Beef Omelette in Red Wine Butter
Potatoes Sautéed in Duck Fat
Insalata Misticanza
Country-Style Baked Apples

A SUNDAY SUPPER BY THE FIRE

his menu conjures up warm thoughts of a relaxed dinner to celebrate, perhaps, the first fire of autumn. Enjoy it with family or friends after doing whatever you like to do on an autumn Sunday--rake leaves, take an outing with the children or, maybe, just read the newspaper! The food should not take you all day to prepare.

The crisp and tangy Insalata Misticanza is redolent of fresh herbs and goat cheese. The greens may be cleaned ahead of time and kept ready for the salad bowl. Dan's Scallion-Beef Omelette in a wine sauce is love at first bite! And if you have never encountered potatoes sautéed in chicken or duck fat then you have a treat in store. Just be sure to save room for the Country-Style Baked Apples, which are baked gently with maple syrup, peach jam and pecans. This is heart warming food at its best!

Enjoy your omelette with a Northwest Pinot Noir or a French Burgundy, then relax near the fire with your baked apple and a steaming mug of freshly brewed coffee. Here's to an autumn Sunday! (And remember, your diet starts...tomorrow!!)

Diane f Morgan

Here we offer a recipe born of desperation one night when there was little in our refrigerator except a few eggs, some scallions and a small piece of leftover roast beef. We improvised and felt the results were worth passing along! This is equally good with leftover lamb, by the way; in either case you will have more tender results if your leftover meat is rare to medium rare.

For 6 servings.

2 cups dry red wine

2 cups good meat stock or light beef broth

2 sticks (8 ounces) *unsalted* butter, cut in tablespoon size pieces

1/2 to 3/4 pound cooked rare beef

6 scallions (green onions)

12 large eggs, beaten lightly with a little freshly ground black pepper

2 tablespoons butter or clarified butter per omelette

A little chopped fresh parsley for garnish, if you wish

SCALLION-BEEF OMELETTE IN RED WINE BUTTER

Twenty minutes before serving, place the wine and stock or broth in a non-aluminum saucepan and bring to a boil. While the mixture is boiling cut the meat into matchstick size pieces and thinly slice the scallions. Have serving plates in a warm but not hot oven.

When the wine-stock mixture has reduced to about 1/4 cup, (turn the oven off), add the butter to the pan and allow to boil until the butter has been absorbed (emulsified) into the liquids. Remove from the heat immediately and fold in the julienned meat. Portion onto your serving plates and hold in the oven while you make the omelettes.

We think the omelettes are best made individually rather than as one giant creation. If you agree, have your guests at the table as you begin preparing them. They cook very quickly.

Heat a 7- or 8-inch omelette pan until hot, then add the butter. When the foam subsides (if you are using non-clarified butter) pour in 2 beaten eggs, or 1/6 of the total mixture. When a skin forms on the bottom of the eggs, in about 5 to 10 seconds, give the mixture a quick stir with a fork. Cook another few seconds to obtain a new bottom skin. Add 1/6 of the sliced scallions over the eggs. Now, using your skill with the pan or a heatproof rubber spatula, fold over the top of the omelette. Allow the bottom to brown lightly for a few seconds, then turn and brown lightly on the other side. The omelette should still be creamy in the center at this point!

Slide the omelette onto a plate on top of the beef-sauce mixture and garnish with the parsley, if desired. Serve at once and begin the second omelette. Repeat for each guest.

To serve 6 persons:

6 to 8 medium red potatoes

4 to 6 tablespoons rendered duck or chicken fat (or clarified butter if you prefer)

Salt and freshly ground black pepper, to taste

1 to 2 tablespoons minced parsley, for garnish

POTATOES SAUTÉED IN DUCK FAT

Bring a large pot of water to a boil. Add 1 tablespoon salt. Add the potatoes, unpeeled, and cook for 8 or more minutes. They should remain firm but be partially cooked. Drain and cool slightly, then cut into wedges or thick slices.

Heat the fat in a large, heavy skillet. Add the potatoes and sauté over medium heat until browned and crisp on all sides, probably about 20 to 30 minutes. (Start these before your wine and stock reduction if you are serving them with the omelette in this menu.) Drain on paper towels, season with the salt and pepper, and serve sprinkled with the parsley if you wish.

NOTE: See the recipe for Chicken Liver Paté (Jewish Style), (p. 118) for directions on making chicken fat. Duck fat can be prepared similarly.

To serve 6:

6 ounces goat cheese, cut into 6 slices

6 tablespoons olive oil

6 fresh basil leaves

2 sprigs fresh thyme

1 sweet red pepper

1 head romaine lettuce

1 head radicchio lettuce

1/2 pound Belgian endive

1 cup thinly sliced fennel bulb (or celery if necessary)

Juice of 1/2 lemon, about 2 tablespoons

2 teaspoons red wine vinegar

4 tablespoons olive oil

Salt and pepper, to taste

INSALATA MISTICANZA

Marinate the cheese slices in the oil and herbs overnight.

Char the skin of the pepper by holding it over a flame or placing it under a broiler until the skin is black. Place the pepper in a plastic bag for 10 to 20 minutes to "steam." Remove from the bag and scrape off the skin; remove the top and the seeds. Cut the pepper into small matchsticks and set aside.

Reserve 6 large romaine leaves for plate liners. Tear the remainder into bite-size pieces. Tear the radicchio into bite-size pieces as well. Cut the endive into 1/4 inch thick rounds, separate the rings and discard the core. Toss these together with the fennel or celery. Blend the lemon juice, vinegar, olive oil and a little salt and pepper. Taste and adjust seasonings if necessary. Toss with the salad. Portion onto the reserved romaine leaves on the salad plates.

Heat 2 tablespoons of oil from the cheese marinade in a small sauté pan and warm the goat cheese over low heat for a minute on each side. Place a round of cheese on each salad and garnish with the red pepper.

6 large apples, either Golden Delicious, Pippin, Granny Smith or Gravenstein

1/2 cup peach or apricot jam

1/3 cup maple syrup

1 teaspoon grated lemon zest

1/3 cup pecans, chopped into small pieces

3 tablespoons butter, cut into 6 pieces

COUNTRY-STYLE BAKED APPLES

Preheat oven to 375º.

Wash the apples and core them neatly from end to end, using either an apple corer or a small, sharp knife. You want a clean, round opening all the way through the apple core.

With the point of a small, sharp knife make a horizontal incision about 1/4 inch deep all the way around each apple about 1/3 of the way down the side of the apple. During the baking process the apple skin expands and the skin about this line will act like a lid and lift. This allows steam to escape and prevents the apple from bursting.

Place the apples in a baking dish that closely fits them, allowing 1 inch of space between each apple. Combine the jam, maple syrup and lemon zest, mix well, and drizzle evenly over the apples. Most of it should go inside the fruit, a little should be drizzled on the outside surface. Sprinkle the pecan pieces evenly inside the apples and top with a piece of butter. You may prepare the recipe up to this point and hold at room temperature for 1 to 2 hours if you like.

Bake in a preheated 375º oven for 15 to 20 minutes, basting twice during this time. Cook for another 20 to 30 minutes or until a knife inserted at the incision slips in easily. Allow to cool for 10 minutes before serving.

DM

Chicken Liver Paté (Jewish Style)
Homemade Corned Beef
Cranberry Chutney
Diane's Mustard Sauce
Lemon Marmalade
Candied Oranges Dipped in Chocolate
Chocolate Grand Marnier Truffles
Golden Savory Almonds

FOODS FOR GIVING

 his is a special section meant for special people--those for whom you do not know what to buy, those who love to cook for themselves or simply anyone deserving of your time and efforts. Ask any food lover what gifts he treasures and you will likely hear that gifts of food are the most enjoyed!

I remember one occasion when we were entertaining a large group of friends. We had cooked for days and were ready to enjoy our guests as they arrived. One couple surprised us with a loaf of lemon-walnut bread which we tucked away in a safe place overnight. The next morning we awoke bleary-eyed to enjoy the wonderful homemade bread with a pot of tea and some fresh fruit. Now that was a special gift!

We have included here all sorts of food appropriate for giving as gifts. There is a Chicken Liver Paté, Homemade Corned Beef, Lemon Marmalade, and Cranberry Chutney. For your chocoholic friends there are Chocolate Grand Marnier Truffles and Candied Oranges Dipped in Chocolate. My Golden Savory Almonds are a snap to make and always are welcomed. The Mustard Sauce is a favorite of mine and would be wonderful with the corned beef.

So the next time you are faced with a gift to give or an extra long Christmas list, think about how much more fun it would be to spend time in your kitchen instead of at the shopping mall!

Diane J. Morgan

CHICKEN LIVER PATÉ (JEWISH STYLE)

The problem with writing a cookbook with cohorts is that one must divulge certain recipes which could otherwise remain secret! My liver paté is one of them. I find it hard to admit that I put saltine crackers in this recipe, but I have served it at many catered parties and to paté-loving friends. It always gets requests for more!

To serve 8 to 10 as an appetizer:

1 medium onion, minced

3 tablespoons rendered chicken fat, divided

1 pound chicken livers, cut in half

6 saltine crackers

3/4 teaspoon Lawry seasoning

2 tablespoons Hungarian sweet paprika

Pinch sugar

Freshly ground black pepper, to taste

Pinch kosher salt

2 large eggs, hard boiled, peeled and cut into quarters

In a sauté pan large enough to hold all the livers without crowding, sauté the onion in 1 tablespoon of the fat over medium heat until soft and translucent, about 4 minutes. Raise the heat to medium high and add the livers, browning them quickly while stirring occasionally. Season with some salt and pepper.

While the livers are still slightly pink on the inside, remove all contents of the pan to the workbowl of a food processor fitted with the metal blade. Purée the liver-onion mixture, scraping down the bowl as necessary.

Add the remaining 2 tablespoons of chicken fat, the crackers, the seasonings and the eggs. Process until smooth. The texture should be firm and smooth, not stiff or dry. Add a little more chicken fat if necessary to correct dryness.

Taste and adjust the seasonings. Pack into an oiled decorative mold or crock. Seal tightly and refrigerate at least 4 hours before serving.

Remove from the refrigerator 20 minutes before serving. Serve with toast rounds, French bread or your favorite crackers.

NOTE: If chicken fat is not available at your market you can make it easily! Make a batch of unseasoned chicken stock and refrigerate it overnight. The solidified fat you find on top the next day is just rendered chicken fat ready for using. Or buy chicken fat pieces from your butcher and melt them slowly in a heavy bottomed skillet over low heat until melted completely. Strain and store in the freezer. Keeps indefinitely.

DM

Ingredients

1 beef brisket, about 6 to 7 pounds, trimmed

1/2 cup kosher salt

3 tablespoons brown sugar

1 tablespoon dried rosemary

3 small bay leaves

3/4 teaspoon dried thyme

1 teaspoon dried sage

1 teaspoon cracked black pepper

1 teaspoon ground coriander

4 cloves garlic, thinly sliced

2 teaspoons whole mustard seed

1 teaspoon whole allspice

1 teaspoon whole black pepper

HOMEMADE CORNED BEEF

Corned Beef is meat which has been cured by the chemical action of salt and sugar and whatever seasonings the cook cares to use. Sometimes a brine solution is made and the meat submerged in it; otherwise, as in this case, the curing mixture is rubbed into the meat which is then placed in a shallow dish or sealed in a heavy plastic bag. There is no saltpeter (sodium nitrate) in this recipe, so expect the meat to be a brown color rather than the commercial red color. Plan to let the cure work for 10 to 25 days before cooking. The longer you cure the meat the spicier its flavor, but it is best to cook it by the end of the fourth week. Before cooking, soak the meat in several changes of cold water for 1 to 2 days. To braise the meat, place it in a stovetop casserole and cover the meat with boiling water. Simmer, covered, until it is fork tender, allowing about 20-30 minutes per pound.

Select a glass or ceramic baking dish large enough to hold the meat in one layer; use two dishes if necessary.

In an electric spice grinder, blender or food processor, grind together the salt, sugar, rosemary, bay leaves, thyme, sage, pepper and coriander. Rub this mixture evenly into all sides of the meat, including the ends and crevices.

Lay the garlic slices in the bottom of the dish and sprinkle on the mustard seed, whole allspice, and whole pepper.

Lay the meat on top of the seasonings. Cover tightly with plastic wrap and refrigerate. A few hours after rubbing in the cure, the meat will exude some liquid, then eventually will re-absorb most of it. This is an indication that the cure is working. Turn the meat daily until you are ready to soak and cook it.

CRANBERRY CHUTNEY

4 cups whole cranberries (fresh or frozen)

2 1/2 cups sugar

1 1/4 cups water

6 whole cloves

2 cinnamon sticks

1 teaspoon kosher salt

2 tart apples (preferably Pippin or Granny Smith), peeled, cored and diced

2 firm pears, peeled, cored and diced

1 small onion, diced

1 cup golden raisins

1/3 cup chopped dried apricots

1/2 cup hazelnuts, toasted, skins removed, then chopped

2 teaspoons grated lemon zest

Try this chutney instead of the usual cranberry sauce with the holiday turkey or goose. It is a favorite food gift of mine. This recipes makes about 2 quarts.

In a large, deep saucepan combine the first six ingredients. Bring to a boil, stirring frequently, and cook 10 to 15 minutes, or until the berries pop. Add the apples, pears, onion, raisins and apricots and continue cooking, stirring frequently, until thick. This may take up to 15 minutes. Remove from the heat and add the hazelnuts and lemon zest. Discard the cinnamon sticks and cloves, if you can find them. Ladle into sterilized canning jars and process in a boiling water bath for 10 minutes. Alternatively, the chutney will keep under refrigeration for up to 6 months.

DM

DIANE'S MUSTARD SAUCE

For 2 cups of sauce:

1 2-ounce can Coleman's dry mustard

1 cup sugar

2 teaspoons kosher salt

1 teaspoon cornstarch

1/2 cup cider vinegar

1/4 cup dry white wine

1 whole egg, beaten

In a non-aluminum, heavy-bottomed saucepan mix the mustard, sugar, salt and cornstarch. Stir in the vinegar and wine, then the egg.

Cook, stirring constantly with a whisk, over *low* heat until thickened, not over 160º on an instant read thermometer.

Pour into decorative jars and, when it has cooled, refrigerate. Keeps up to 1 month refrigerated.

This recipe may be doubled.

DM

2 large or 3 medium lemons

5 cups water

2 1/4 cups sugar

LEMON MARMALADE

Cut a 1/2 inch slice from each end of each lemon and discard. Cut the lemons in half lengthwise. With the cut side down, slice the lemons crosswise as thinly as possible.

Collect the juice and slices, discarding the seeds, and put into a 2-cup measure. You need 1 1/2 cups.

In a non-aluminum, heavy-bottomed, 3 1/2 quart saucepan bring the lemons, juice, and water to a boil. Boil gently, uncovered, for 30 minutes.

Strain into a 4-cup measure. Add water to bring the liquid level to 3 cups if necessary. Place the fruit, 3 cups of liquid and the sugar in the pan. Bring to a boil, stirring occasionally, and boil until a candy thermometer registers 220º. This will take about 30 to 35 minutes. Remove from the heat.

Test the marmalade by placing a teaspoon of the mixture on a chilled plate. Put the plate in the freezer for a few minutes. If the marmalade does not run when you tip the plate then it is thick enough. It should be a pale lemon yellow and the liquid clear looking.

Ladle the hot marmalade into 3 hot, sterilized 1-cup canning jars. Have the lids hot. Wipe the rims of the jars, put the lids in place, screw on the bands, and turn upside-down for 5 minutes. Turn rightside-up and let sit undisturbed until the lid pops. They will be sealed at this point.

DM

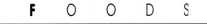

4 Valencia oranges

2 cups water

3 1/2 cups sugar

Another 3 cups sugar, or as needed, for coating

2 pounds semisweet coating chocolate, chopped into small pieces. Reserve a 2 ounce chunk.

CANDIED ORANGES DIPPED IN CHOCOLATE

Cut the oranges in half lengthwise. With the cut side down slice the oranges crosswise into 1/4 inch pieces. Discard the ends.

In a 10-inch sauté pan combine the water and the 3 1/2 cups of sugar. Stir to blend, then bring to a boil over medium heat.

Add the orange slices, separating them, and simmer them *gently* for 1 hour uncovered. Periodically dunk any floating slices. Remove from the heat and cool to room temperature.

Remove the orange slices, with a slotted spoon and transfer to a cooling rack set over a baking sheet to let drain and dry for 24 hours.

After drying the slices, toss them in the granulated sugar and reserve them. Do not stack them or let them stick together.

While you are coating the orange slices, have the chocolate melting slowly in the top of a double boiler over 120° water. Add water occasionally to maintain that temperature.

When all the chocolate is melted and creamy and registers 100° on an instant read thermometer, remove the top section of the double boiler. Add the 2-ounce chunk of reserved chocolate and stir gently until the thermometer reads 88 to 91 degrees, then remove what remains of the chunk of chocolate.

Now dip the orange slices 2/3 of the way into the chocolate. Gently scrape off excess chocolate against the side of the pan and set on a sheet of wax paper to set. Work quickly with the slices. If the chocolate becomes too thick for dipping, place it over the 120° water again until it has reached 88 to 91°.

DM

CHOCOLATE GRAND MARNIER TRUFFLES

These are for bittersweet chocolate lovers.

3/4 cup heavy cream

12 ounces semisweet chocolate, melted

2 1/2 tablespoons Grand Marnier

1 stick (4 ounces) unsalted butter, at room temperature

1/4 cup plus 2 tablespoons Droste cocoa

1 1/2 teaspoons cinnamon

Heat the cream to a boil. Add the melted chocolate and whisk until smooth.   Cool to room temperature.

In the meantime, thoroughly combine the cocoa and cinnamon in a small bowl and set aside.

When the chocolate mixture has cooled, add the Grand Marnier and whisk to combine.

Beat the butter into the chocolate mixture, bit by bit, until it is completely incorporated. Chill, covered, until firm--at least 8 hours.

Shape the mixture into balls, 1 1/2 inches in diameter. Roll each in a plate of the cocoa-cinnamon mixture. You may want to roll them twice for a thorough coating.

Pack in layers in an airtight container and refrigerate or freeze. They will keep for several months.

Makes about 40 truffles.

DM

GOLDEN SAVORY ALMONDS

For about 5 cups:

2 egg whites

1 1/2 tablespoons dijon mustard

1/4 teaspoon cayenne

1/2 teaspoon sugar

4 cups raw (unblanched) almonds, about 20 ounces

2/3 cup freshly grated parmesan cheese

1 1/2 teaspoons kosher salt

Preheat the oven to 300º. In a mixing bowl whisk the egg whites until they are frothy. Add the mustard, cayenne and sugar, and whisk until incorporated. Add the almonds and toss them to coat evenly. Place the nuts in a colander and toss again to remove excess coating.

Wipe out the mixing bowl. In it place the parmesan and salt and mix well. Add the nuts and toss until all the seasoning has been picked up.

Distribute the nuts between two non-stick or parchment lined baking sheets. Bake for 25 minutes or until nicely browned. Toss every 10 minutes. Turn off the oven and leave the nuts inside for 30 more minutes. Cool completely.

These may be frozen in an airtight container. Bring to room temperature before serving.

DM

Cream of Chestnut Soup
Duck Breasts Au Porto
Purée of Celery Root
Salad with Lemon Vinaigrette
Pear Tart Tatin

A FRENCH DINNER FOR FOOD-LOVING FRIENDS

What could be more enjoyable on a cold winter evening than a gathering of good friends for a great meal! Here is a sophisticated menu for a special occasion, but the food would be just as good-tasting at a casual get-together! Cream of Chestnut Soup is rich but easy to make; Duck Breasts Au Porto are paired with Purée of Celery Root; Salad with Lemon Vinaigrette follows the entrée as is sometimes done in France; and the Pear Tart Tatin might just make you beg for mercy! The food is rich and full flavored, so just space out the courses a little while enjoying good friends who love good food!

Audrey Urbonovich

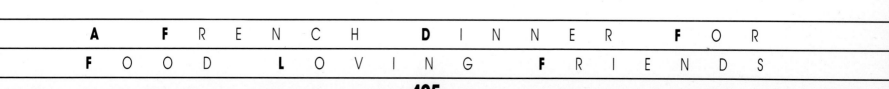

1 medium onion, coarsely chopped

1 medium carrot, coarsely chopped

1/2 rib celery, coarsely chopped

1 tablespoon unsalted butter (or use rendered duck or chicken fat)

3 to 4 cups chicken or veal stock, preferably homemade

1/4 cup dry white wine

15 ounces unsweetened chestnut purée

1/4 to 1/2 cup heavy cream

2 tablespoons brandy

1/2 teaspoon salt, or to taste

1/4 teaspoon freshly ground black pepper

1/4 teaspoon freshly grated nutmeg

4 tablespoons finely chopped parsley

CREAM OF CHESTNUT SOUP

This is a very rich first course so small portions are advised! I always think of it as the beginning of a festive meal, like a New Year's Eve dinner. Anyway, it is definitely a winter soup.

In a heavy, medium-sized pot, cook the chopped vegetables in the butter until they are soft but not browned.

Add the stock and wine and bring to a boil, then reduce to a simmer and cook for 10 to 15 minutes. Remove from the heat and cool slightly.

Strain the solids from the soup and reserve them, and the liquid! In a food processor or blender fitted with the metal blade, purée the vegetables, adding liquid if necessary. Add the chestnut purée, and, with the machine running, pour about half the liquid through the feed tube and process until the mixture is smooth.

Return the puréed mixture and all remaining liquid to the cleaned pot and heat through. Add 1/4 cup of the cream, the brandy and the seasonings. Taste and adjust the seasonings to your liking. If the soup seems too thick, add the remaining cream. Serve very hot in small bowls and garnish with the parsley.

NOTE: If you have used canned broth or bouillon cubes, taste the soup before adding *any* salt--you probably will not need any!

Ask your butcher to bone the breasts for you if you are not so inclined! This recipe uses only the breasts, wingtips and necks; be sure to save the legs for other meals and the carcasses for making stock. If you have no homemade stock for this meal, please choose a good quality canned broth rather than bouillon cubes, which are extremely salty.

Wingtips and necks from 3 ducks

DUCK BREASTS AU PORTO

Chop the wingtips and necks into small pieces with a large, heavy knife or meat cleaver.

Heat 1 tablespoon of the fat in a heavy saucepan and add the chopped wingtips and necks. Brown on all sides, then drain the fat. Add the chicken stock, bring to a boil, and then simmer over medium heat until it is reduced to 1 cup of stock. Strain and reserve the stock. Discard the bones.

Heat the remaining 2 tablespoons of fat in a large, heavy skillet. Over medium high heat sauté the duck breasts about 3-4 minutes on each side, until they are medium rare, about 130º on an instant read

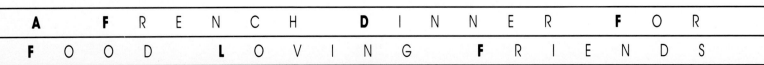

3 tablespoons rendered duck or chicken fat, or oil of your choice, divided

2 cups chicken stock, homemade is best

6 duck breast halves, boned out of 3 ducks, and skinned

Salt and freshly ground black pepper, to taste

6 tablespoons tawny port, good quality non-vintage

1 large clove garlic, minced

1/2 large shallot, minced

1/4 teaspoon dried thyme or 1/2 teaspoon fresh, minced

1/4 teaspoon dried tarragon or 1/2 teaspoon fresh, minced

1 to 3 teaspoons fresh lemon juice

3 tablespoons unsalted butter, cut in 1 tablespoon pieces

thermometer. Do not cook them until all the pinkness is gone! If they brown too heavily before the interior is done, place the pan in a 400º oven to finish the cooking. Season lightly with salt and pepper and keep warm.

Discard the fat in the pan. Heat the pan again over medium high heat, then add 2 tablespoons of the port, scraping up any browned bits in the bottom of the pan. Add the garlic and shallot and cook 1 minute, then add the reserved stock and cook it until only 1/2 cup remains. Add the remaining port, the herbs and the lemon juice by the teaspoonful until it balances the sweetness of the port to your taste. Adjust for salt and pepper if necessary.

Lower heat to medium low. Swirl in the butter until it disappears and begins to thicken the sauce. Immediately pour over the warm duck breasts and serve.

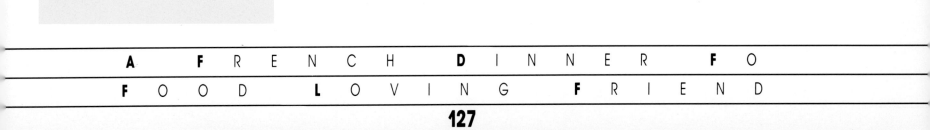

Serves 6

1 large celery root, about 1 to 1 1/2 pounds

1 medium russet potato, about 6 ounces

1/4 to 1/2 cup heavy cream

4 ounces unsalted butter, cut in 1 tablespoon pieces, at room temperature

1 teaspoon salt

Freshly ground black pepper

4 tablespoons freshly squeezed lemon juice

2 tablespoons white wine vinegar

1 tablespoon dijon mustard

1 tablespoon sugar

1/4 teaspoon salt

1/4 teaspoon freshly ground black pepper

8 to 10 tablespoons good quality olive oil

2 tablespoons minced scallions

1 tablespoon capers

2 heads butter lettuce

PURÉE OF CELERY ROOT

Peel the celery root carefully and cut into roughly 1-inch dice.

Peel the potato and cut into the same size dice.

Bring water to a boil in a 3- to 4-quart saucepan. Add the vegetables and boil them, partially covered, until they are quite tender, about 15 minutes. Drain well.

In a food processor fitted with the metal blade, purée the vegetables while they are still hot; add the butter piece by piece until it is just incorporated. Add enough cream so that the purée is the consistency you like. Season with salt and pepper to your taste and serve.

This can be kept warm in a very low oven for 30 minutes if necessary. If you need to hold it longer press a piece of plastic wrap directly on the surface of the purée and refrigerate. Reheat gently in a double boiler over simmering water.

SALAD WITH LEMON VINAIGRETTE

This is a very light, slightly sweet dressing. I recommend serving this salad after the entrée, in the French manner. It serves as a refreshing counterpoint to such a rich and sumptuous menu.

Combine the lemon juice, vinegar, mustard, sugar, salt, and pepper in a small bowl or in the workbowl of a food processor. Use a whisk to combine ingredients well if you are not using a processor. Run the food processor for 20 seconds to blend the ingredients, and, with the machine running, pour in a thin stream of the oil, gradually pouring faster until all is incorporated. Do the same if working by hand. Add the scallions and process a few seconds. Taste and adjust the seasonings with sugar or lemon juice, if necessary, and/or salt and pepper. Place in an airtight storage container and add the capers. Refrigerate until ready to use.

Wash and dry the lettuce. Tear it into fairly large-size pieces. If you are preparing the lettuce ahead of time, wrap it inside a clean towel and place in a large plastic bag. Refrigerate.

Toss the greens and dressing in a large bowl just before serving. Serves 6.

PASTRY

1 cup all purpose unbleached flour

4 ounces unsalted butter, cut in tablespoon size pieces, *frozen*

1 tablespoon sugar

Pinch of salt

2 to 3 tablespoons ice water

FILLING

4 ounces unsalted butter

3/4 cup sugar

5 to 6 almost ripe pears, peeled, cored and quartered (choose ripe Bosc pears or slightly underripe Comice pears)

TOPPING

1 cup heavy cream

2 tablespoons sugar

1/2 teaspoon vanilla extract

PEAR TART TATIN

To make the pastry place the flour, butter, sugar, and salt in the workbowl of a food processor fitted with the metal blade. Pulse several times, until the butter is between the size of peas and lima beans on the average.

With the machine running pour in the ice water and run for 3 or 4 seconds, then stop the machine. If you can squeeze a handful of granules into a dough you have added enough water. If the dough seems too loose then, with the machine running, add more water a teaspoon at a time until the dough texture suits you. Flatten the pastry into a 5-inch disc, wrap airtight and refrigerate.

Preheat the oven to 375º. Choose a good quality, dependable 9- or 10-inch ovenproof skillet with either a non-stick coating or a well-seasoned surface.

Over medium low heat, melt the butter in the pan. Sprinkle in the sugar and cook slowly until it dissolves, about 7 to 10 minutes.

Arrange the pear quarters neatly in concentric circles in the pan; *this will be the top when you are finished!* Fill in with remaining pears, cutting smaller pieces to fit if necessary. Cook over medium low heat for 10 to 15 minutes, swirling occasionally to prevent sticking.

If the pastry disc is too firm to roll out, then let it sit at room temperature for a few minutes during the early cooking of the pears. Roll out the pastry on a lightly floured board until it measures about 1 inch larger than the edge of the pan. It need not be exact. Working quickly, drape the pastry over the pears and fold over the extra pastry so that the edge is a double thickness.

Place the pan on a pizza pan or jelly roll pan to catch any drips and place on the middle level of the preheated oven. Bake 40 to 45 minutes.

Remove from the oven and return the skillet to a burner. Cook over low heat for 5 to 15 minutes to further thicken the juices; they should become syrupy--the time will vary with the fruit. When the juices appear thick as you tip the pan from side to side turn the heat off. Place your serving plate inverted over the pan and, in one graceful movement, flip the tart onto the serving plate! Any pieces remaining in the pan may be inserted where needed to make the tart look whole.

Whip the cream with the sugar and vanilla until it stands in very soft peaks. Serve the tart warm with a spoonful of the whipped cream. This will serve 6 to 8 persons.

GRAPE-GIN FIZZ

In an 8-ounce glass place several cubes of ice.

Pour over 1 ounce (2 tablespoons) of gin.

Add 2 ounces (1/4 cup) of unsweetened white grape juice.

Squeeze 1 wedge of lime and add to the glass.

Add 2 to 3 ounces of seltzer water.

Stir and serve.

If you like lime juice and tequila combined as a margarita, then try this easy drink. The combination of gin with its slight juniper flavor, lime juice, unsweetened grape juice and carbonated water produces a very refreshing apertif.

SLICED PAPAYA WITH RASPBERRY SAUCE

The night before serving prepare the sauce. Purée the raspberries in a food processor or blender until smooth, then sieve to remove the seeds. In a medium-sized mixing bowl combine the raspberries, lime juice, sugar and salt. Stir until the sugar dissolves. Taste and adjust with more lime juice or sugar, if needed. Refrigerate covered.

Bring the sauce to room temperature before serving.

To serve, place 2 to 3 tablespoons of sauce on a salad-size plate. Carefully lay the papaya slices on top, fanning them decoratively. Serve immediately.

NOTE: You may slice the papaya up to 1 hour in advance. Reserve it covered, at room temperature. Use any remaining sauce as a topping for ice cream or other fruit, such as pears.

For 6 servings:

2 12-ounce packages whole, slightly sweetened raspberries, thawed

2 1/2 tablespoons fresh lime juice

3 1/2 tablespoons powdered sugar

Pinch salt

3 ripe papayas, peeled, halved, seeded, and thinly sliced

WAFFLES

2 egg whites, at room temperature

1 1/2 cups all purpose unbleached flour

2 teaspoons baking powder

1 1/2 cups milk

1/4 cup melted butter

2 large eggs

3 medium scallions, minced

1 cup freshly grated parmesan cheese

3/4 cup finely crumbled Oregon, Maytag or other good quality blue cheese

WAFFLE TOPPING

12 slices good bacon, cooked crisply and crumbled, fat reserved

2 pounds fresh mushrooms, thinly sliced

1 bunch scallions, thinly sliced

2 ounces dried porcini mushrooms, soaked in hot water until soft, drained (reserve the liquid) and rinsed well to remove any sand

1 1/2 cups port wine, ruby or tawny

1/2 cup of the finely *strained* porcini liquid

3 tablespoons heavy cream

Salt and freshly ground black pepper, to taste

BLUE CHEESE WAFFLES WITH MUSHROOMS AND BACON

These wonderful, savory waffles are topped with a full flavored mushroom mixture. A great deal of that flavor results from the use of dried porcini mushrooms imported from Italy. They are not inexpensive but a small amount goes a long way! If you are not able to find the porcini then dried Polish or domestic mushrooms are reasonable substitutes.

Beat the egg whites until stiff but not dry.

In a large mixing bowl stir together the flour and baking powder. Stir in the remaining waffle ingredients (except the beaten egg whites) and combine well.

Using a large rubber spatula, fold in the beaten egg whites gently.

Bake in a waffle iron according to the manufacturer's directions. Yields about 4 large square waffles or approximately 16 3-inch segments. You may make them in advance, freeze and reheat them; they will be even crispier in that case.

In a sauté pan heat several tablespoons of the bacon fat and cook the fresh mushrooms and scallions until wilted. Chop the porcinis and add to the pan. Add the port and the 1/2 cup of reserved and strained porcini liquid. Cook until most of the liquid has evaporated. Stir in the cream, taste for seasonings and use to top the warmed waffles. Sprinkle the crumbled bacon over the waffles and serve.

K. T.

2 tablespoons butter

1 or 2 cloves garlic, cut in half

12 very thin slices red or sweet yellow onion

12 thin slices fresh, ripe tomato

A little fresh basil, if available

Salt and freshly ground black pepper, to taste

6 large eggs

6 tablespoons heavy cream

6 tablespoons grated Gruyère or Emmenthaler cheese

SHIRRED EGGS

Preheat the oven to 375º. Pick a shallow baking dish which will hold 6 small (6-ounce) ramekins comfortably. Have 4 cups of water simmering on the range to prepare a water bath.

Spread 1 teaspoon of butter all around the inside of each ramekin. Rub each ramekin well with the cut side of a piece of garlic.

Place 2 thin slices of onion, then 2 thin slices of tomato in each ramekin. Top with a little fresh basil if available.

Place the ramekins in the baking pan and add simmering water to come halfway up the outsides of the ramekins. Place in the oven and bake about 5 minutes, until the onion is transparent and the tomato begins to soften. Remove from the oven and season with the salt and pepper. Break an egg into each ramekin and return to the oven for about 8 minutes, until the egg white begins to set. Spoon 1 tablespoon of the cream over each egg and sprinkle with 1 tablespoon of the cheese. Bake about 5 minutes more, until the eggs are just set and the cheese is melted. *Be sure to test for doneness!* Baked eggs always appear not to be done when they really are--poke them, do not just look!

These gooey, spicy rolls are a specialty of the Pennsylvania Dutch in south-eastern Pennsylvania where I grew up. My children always called them "upside-down rolls" because they are made like pineapple upside-down cake!

GEORGIA'S PHILADELPHIA STICKY BUNS

Preheat oven to 150º and then *turn off.*

Place the yeast in a 2-cup glass measuring cup. Pour the lukewarm milk over the yeast and add 1 teaspoon of the sugar. Let stand for 15 minutes, then stir thoroughly to dissolve yeast. Stir in the eggs and vanilla.

For 12 to 16 buns in a 9x13 inch pan:

1 tablespoon active dry yeast

1 cup milk, scalded and cooled to lukewarm (not over 115°)

1/2 cup granulated sugar, divided

2 eggs, beaten

1 teaspoon vanilla extract

3 to 4 cups all purpose unbleached or bread flour

1 teaspoon salt

1/2 cup unsalted butter, melted

1 teaspoon cinnamon

3/4 cup dark brown sugar, packed

1/2 cup chopped pecans

If you are using a food processor, place the flour, salt and 1/4 cup of the granulated sugar in the workbowl fitted with the dough blade if so equipped. Stir the yeast mixture and slowly pour it into the workbowl while the machine is running. If you hear "sloshing" you are pouring too fast! Have some extra flour on the counter just in case your dough is too sticky and cannot rotate inside the workbowl. When the dough ball has formed and is rotating, allow the machine to run 45 to 60 seconds to knead the dough.

If you are using a mixer, place the liquids in the bowl and fit the machine with the pastry paddle to speed the dough formation. Add about 1/2 the total flour and run on slow speed to obtain a batter-like consistency. Now remove the paddle and fit the dough hook and continue adding flour until a dough ball forms. Continue kneading for about 4 to 6 more minutes. The dough should clean the sides of the bowl.

Place the dough in a gallon-size plastic bag (lightly floured if you wish), squeeze out all the air and place a wire twist at the *top* of the bag so that the dough has room to expand in the bag. Place on a potholder on the oven shelf until it has doubled in size, about 1 to 1 1/2 hours. Open the bag, press down the dough, squeeze out the air and reseal at the top. Put it back in the oven for a second rising until it has doubled again.

Remove the dough from the bag and pat or roll it into an approximately 10x16 rectangle. Melt 3 tablespoons of the butter and brush over the dough, leaving a 1-inch strip along one of the long sides unbuttered.

Mix the remaining 1/4 cup of granulated sugar with the cinnamon and sprinkle over the buttered portion of the dough. Roll up the dough from the buttered long side like a jelly roll. Melt the remaining butter in the bottom of the baking pan, coating evenly. Sprinkle the brown sugar over the butter, then the pecans.

Cut the dough into 1 inch slices and arrange in the pan. Cover with buttered or oiled plastic wrap and allow to double or even nearly triple in size.

Preheat oven to 375°. Remove plastic carefully from the pan and bake the rolls 20 to 25 minutes until the tops are nicely browned. The internal temperature of the dough should be at least 180° on an instant read thermometer.

Invert onto a platter and scrape any remaining syrup from the pan over the rolls.

Spaghetti with Papaya and Caviar
Tournedos Taggart
Snow Peas with Shallots and Basil
Simple French Rolls
My Favorite Cheesecake with Chocolate and Strawberries

A SPECIAL VALENTINE

*L*et's hear it for life's little excuses to celebrate--when you can find the tiniest reason to pull out a few stops. Valentine's Day is as good an excuse as any; after all, tradition dictates that we ought to do something special for our sweeties. What could be more special than a marvelous gift from the kitchen?

Our menu begins with an unusual pasta for a first course. I have mixed fresh egg spaghetti with butter and lemon, added sweet ripe papaya and topped the whole with glistening black caviar. The caviar I use is very exciting because it is very American--Columbia River sturgeon caviar. It is delicious and far less expensive than the imported variety. Regardless of what type of caviar you use, be sure the word "malassol" is included on the label, since this means the caviar is packed fresh and is only very lightly salted. It is perishable, so if for some strange reason you do not use it all, the remainder will freeze very well.

Following the first course is our entrée, a beautiful beef tenderloin steak stuffed with blue cheese, bacon and bread crumbs. These "Tournedos Taggart" are served with a Bearnaise Sauce, easily made in a food processor. A simple sauté of snow peas and herbs complements the steak. Our dinner is completed by Diane's stunning cheesecake, embellished with a bit of chocolate and nestled in brilliant strawberry sauce.

This is a natural "make ahead" meal in several ways: the pasta sauce may be done well before the meal, the papaya is easily cut an hour or so beforehand and the steaks may be stuffed hours prior to serving! The cheesecake, of course, is a natural do-ahead task.

We would suggest a good, dry, sparkling wine with the pasta and a fine, dry, red wine with the beef. Enjoy your evening.

Kathleen Taggart

SPAGHETTI WITH PAPAYA AND CAVIAR

This is an easy, elegant and colorful first course for a special meal. Some fine caviar is now being produced in Oregon and Washington from Columbia River sturgeon roe. Golden American Caviar from Great Lakes whitefish is also a good product, though not as colorful in this dish. Just make sure to buy fresh, not heavily salted caviar.

In a large pot bring 7 to 8 quarts of water to a boil. Toss in a tablespoon of salt after the water boils, then add the noodles and cook until just done (with a bit of bite left--not mushy).

While the pasta is cooking, add the lemon zest, pepper and papaya to the melted butter and warm gently.

When the pasta is cooked and thoroughly drained, put it in a large bowl and toss with the papaya mixture. Divide among 6 heated serving plates and top with a well-rounded 1/2 teaspoon of the caviar. Serve immediately.

K. T.

For 6 servings.

1 pound fresh egg spaghetti

6 tablespoons unsalted butter, melted

Zest of 1 lemon, finely grated

Freshly ground black pepper, to taste

1 small to medium ripe papaya, peeled, seeded and cut into 1/2-inch cubes

About 2 ounces fresh caviar (black in color if possible)

TOURNEDOS TAGGART

In a small bowl or in a food processor, blend the cheese and breadcrumbs until they are smooth. Add the crumbled bacon, stirring just to mix.

In the side of each steak insert a small, sharp knife not quite through to the other side, and carefully angle the knife to one side and then the other to form a pocket in the meat. It may help to insert your finger to gently open up the pocket. Try not to tear through the other side of the steak.

Gently stuff the steaks with the cheese-crumb-bacon mixture. Be patient, they really will take all the stuffing.

Just before cooking salt and pepper the steaks. They may be grilled outdoors if you like. If you are cooking them indoors, heat a large, heavy skillet over moderate heat and add 2 tablespoons vegetable oil. When the oil is hot add the steaks, placing in the pan only as many as comfortably fit. Do not crowd them. Cook until medium rare, about 4 minutes per side.

STEAKS

6 six ounce beef tenderloin steaks

3 ounces good quality blue cheese (such as Roquefort, Oregon Blue, Maytag) at room temperature

4 tablespoons dry bread crumbs

6 strips bacon, cooked crisply and crumbled

Salt and freshly ground black pepper

2 tablespoons vegetable oil

BEARNAISE SAUCE

2 sticks (8 ounces) unsalted butter, melted and kept hot

1 cup dry vermouth or white wine

A few grinds black pepper

2 or 3 tablespoons minced shallots or onion

1 tablespoon fresh parsley

1 tablespoon minced fresh tarragon, or 1 teaspoon dried

3 egg yolks

1 1/2 pounds fresh snow peas

4 tablespoons unsalted butter

2 tablespoons minced shallots or onion

Salt and freshly ground black pepper, to taste

2 tablespoons fresh basil, chopped, or 2 teaspoons dried

While the steaks are cooking make the Bearnaise Sauce. In a small, non-aluminum saucepan, place the wine, pepper, shallots or onion, parsley, and tarragon. Bring to a boil and cook until the mixture has reduced to 2 to 3 tablespoons, almost a syrup.

In the workbowl of a food procesor or blender place the egg yolks and wine mixture. With the machine running slowly pour in the hot butter so that it combines with the egg yolks and the sauce thickens. When all of the butter has been added, taste for seasonings. Adjust salt and pepper and, if necessary, add a little white wine vinegar to raise the acidity a bit.

To serve, place two tablespoons of Bearnaise Sauce in the center of each serving plate. (Have the plates warm.) Place a fillet on top of the sauce and serve immediately.

SNOW PEAS WITH SHALLOTS AND BASIL

Wash the snow peas and remove the crown and tough string on the straighter side of each pod.

Heat the butter in a large, heavy skillet. Cook the shallots gently over medium low heat until they have softened but not browned, about 5 minutes.

Raise the heat to medium high, add the snow peas and cook, stirring constantly with a wooden spoon, until the peas are evenly coated with butter and shallots. They should be a little cooked but still firm.

Season with salt, pepper and basil and serve.

1 1/2 cups cool water, about 60° to 65°

1 tablespoon active dry yeast

3 1/2 cups all purpose unbleached flour

1/2 cup whole wheat flour

2 teaspoons kosher salt

SIMPLE FRENCH ROLLS

Stir the yeast into the water until dissolved.

If you are using a food processor to make the dough, place the flours and salt in the workbowl fitted with the dough blade, if so equipped. Have a little extra flour available in case your dough is too sticky and cannot rotate inside the workbowl. Stir the yeast mixture and, with the machine running, slowly pour the liquid into the workbowl. If you hear "sloshing" you are pouring too quickly. When the dough ball forms and begins regular rotation inside the workbowl, allow the machine to run for 60 to 90 seconds.

If you are using a mixer, place the liquids in the bowl and fit the machine with the pastry paddle. Add the salt and about half the total flour and run on low speed to obtain a batter-like consistency. Remove the paddle, fit the dough hook and continue adding flour until a dough ball forms. Continue kneading for 6 to 8 minutes. The dough should clean the sides of the bowl but be slightly sticky.

Now place the dough in a gallon-size plastic bag, squeeze out all the air and place a wire twist at the *top* of the bag so that the dough will have room to expand. Allow to rise very slowly for about 3 hours. Ideally the room temperature should be about 70°; this is a classic French style dough, a very slow riser!

When the dough has nearly tripled its original size, open the bag, press down the dough, squeeze out all the air, and reseal the bag. Allow the dough to rise (again, in a cool location) until the dough has doubled in size, perhaps 1 to 2 more hours.

When the dough has doubled in size, remove it from the bag, deflate thoroughly and form into 16 or 18 round or oval shapes. Place them on a baking sheet which has been greased, spread with cornmeal or covered with parchment paper. Cover with oiled plastic wrap and let rise again, until double to even triple their original size.

Preheat the oven to 450⁰. Arrange the bottom rack so that it is all the way in the bottom of the oven, if you are using an electric oven. Five minutes before baking place a cakepan or other wide pan with at least 2 inch sides on the bottom shelf (or on the floor of a gas oven) and fill it with boiling water to create steam.

Carefully peel off the plastic wrap from the rolls. Slash them if you like using a very sharp knife or razor blade. Mist them with water from a spray bottle if you have a clean one handy.

Place the pan in the oven on the middle level. Bake for 10 minutes. Carefully remove the water pan. Bake the rolls until they are a beautiful golden brown, probably about 10 more minutes. Timing varies according to the oven, so just keep an eye on the rolls! Cool on a rack and enjoy that wonderful crackling sound crusty bread makes as it cools!

CRUST

1 1/4 cups Post Grapenuts

1/4 cup plus 1 tablespoon granulated sugar

1/4 teaspoon cinnamon

Pinch salt

1/4 cup plus 1 tablespoon melted butter

Optional: 4 ounces semisweet chocolate

FILLING

1 1/2 pounds cream cheese, at room temperature

4 large eggs, at room temperature

1 cup granulated sugar

1 tablespoon pure vanilla extract

1/2 pint (8 ounces) sour cream

SAUCE

2 cups crushed strawberries, fresh or frozen and thawed

2 tablespoons Framboise (raspberry liqueur)

3 tablespoons powdered sugar

MY FAVORITE CHEESECAKE WITH CHOCOLATE AND STRAWBERRIES

Preheat the oven to 375º. In the workbowl of a food processor, or in a blender, grind the Grapenuts until fine crumbs are formed. Allow the machine to run for 2 minutes. Add the sugar, cinnamon and salt and process to combine. Pour in the butter and run just until it is incorporated.

Press the crumbs into a 10-inch springform pan, bringing the crust one inch up the sides of the pan. (I use a 1 cup stainless measuring cup to do this since it helps prevent the corners from being thicker than the sides.)

Bake the crust 10 to 12 minutes until lightly browned and crisp. Cool on a rack. Reduce the oven to 350º.

If you are using the chocolate, melt it and use a rubber spatula to spread it over the bottom of the crust. Put the crust in the freezer to firm the chocolate.

Using a clean food processor workbowl, or with a mixer, process the cream cheese until completely smooth, scraping down the sides once or twice. With the machine stopped, add in, all at once, the eggs, sugar and vanilla. Process until smooth. Add the sour cream to the workbowl and pulse just until incorporated and smooth. The filling must be free of lumps or you will have lumps in the baked filling. Remove the pan from the freezer and gently pour the filling into the pan. The filling will likely come up slightly higher than the crust, which is not a problem.

Place the pan in the center of the oven (now at 350º) and bake for 35 to 40 minutes or until the sides are slightly puffed. The center third of the filling will still be very soft and not set when you shake the pan gently. Turn off the oven and leave the cheesecake in the oven, undisturbed, for 1 hour, then remove and cool on a rack before refrigerating. Leave the cheesecake in the pan during refrigeration. If cracks appear on the surface you baked it a little too long. It will not affect the flavor and you can hide the evidence with a little fresh fruit or whipped cream.

To make the sauce, purée the berries and combine with the Framboise and powdered sugar. Sieve if you wish to remove the seeds. Refrigerate until needed.

To serve, place 2 tablespoons of the sauce on each dessert plate and top with a slice of cheesecake (wipe the knife clean after each cut). If you like, add a slice or half of a strawberry on top of each piece at the crust end for garnish!

DM

SMOKED OYSTERS IN PUFF PASTRY BOUCHÉES

1/2 to 1 1/2 pounds puff pastry, homemade or frozen commercial

1 egg, beaten

FILLING

8 ounces cream cheese, at room temperature

2 to 4 tablespoons heavy cream

1 to 2 tablespoons prepared horseradish

1 to 3 teaspoons freshly squeezed lemon juice

1 tablespoon minced parsley

2 scallions, minced

Salt and freshly ground pepper, to taste

1 3-3/4 ounce tin smoked oysters, drained and cut in thirds

Preheat the oven to 425º. Set the rack in the upper third of the oven. Roll out chilled homemade puff pastry to 1/4 to 1/2 inch, depending on how high you want the shells to be. If you are using frozen commercial puff pastry you may decide to layer 2 or 3 sheets on top of each other since they tend to be very thin and produce very short shells (bouchées). To do this, thaw the sheets slightly, brush the top of the bottom layer with water, gently press on a new layer, and repeat if you like. Our bouchées made from 3 layers of commercial pastry look very nice and stand about 1 to 1 1/4 inches high. Layering the pastry sheets takes more dough, hence the variable weight in the ingredient list!

Cut out bouchées using a 1 1/2 to 2 inch round cutter, fluted if possible. Score each one halfway through, using a 1 inch cutter, centered. This will become the cap.

Remove excess dough from around the bouchées and chill them on cookie sheets 15 to 30 minutes. You may freeze them at this point. Scraps of the pastry can be gathered and rerolled once; beyond that they become very tough.

When ready to bake, lightly brush the *top* of each bouchée with beaten egg. Do not drizzle egg down the sides since they cannot rise as well in that case. Bake in the upper third of the preheated oven, 10 to 12 minutes, or until puffed and golden brown. Cool on a rack. When cool enough to handle, cut out the cap with a small, sharp knife. Reserve the cap and remove any uncooked dough from inside, being careful to leave the bottom intact.

To make the filling, place the cream cheese in the bowl of a food processor fitted with the metal blade. Process until smooth. Add the cream, a tablespoon at a time while the motor is running, until the mixture is about the consistency of mayonnaise. You may not need all the cream. Add the horseradish to taste, then the lemon juice, parsley, scallions, salt, and pepper. Pulse to combine, then taste. Adjust the seasonings with more horseradish, lemon juice or salt and pepper.

Scrape the mixture into a bowl and fold in the smoked oysters. You may refrigerate the filling at this point. Bring back to room temperature before using.

To serve, preheat the oven to 400º. Spoon a little of the filling into each bouchée and cover loosely with a puff pastry cap. Place on a cookie sheet and bake in the middle level of the oven about 10 minutes, or until just heated through and bubbling. Serve immediately.

Makes 60 to 80 depending on how large you make the shells.

PASTRY

4 cups unbleached white pastry flour

2 1/2 sticks (20 tablespoons) unsalted butter, cut into 1/2-inch cubes, very cold or frozen

1 generous teaspoon kosher salt

3/4 cup ice water

A little dijon mustard

FILLING

1 pound low fat cream cheese (Neufchatel), at room temperature

20 ounces feta cheese

5 large eggs

1/2 teaspoon good quality saffron threads

SAVORY SAFFRON CHEESE TART

In the workbowl of a food processor fitted with the metal blade, place the flour, butter and salt. Pulse the machine until the mixture resembles coarse meal. With the machine running, pour in the ice water, taking 5 to 10 seconds to pour. Stop the machine when the dough *just* begins to hold together. *Do not* let it form a ball.

Divide the dough in half. On a well-floured surface roll each half into a circle about 16 to 17 inches in diameter. Place each circle of dough in a greased 12-inch tart pan with a removable bottom. Prick the bottom of the shells well with a fork. Place the two tart shells in the freezer for 30 minutes or until very firm. Meanwhile preheat the oven to 400°.

When the shells are firm remove them from the freezer and line them with aluminum foil, pressing down on the bottom and sides. Fill each shell with pie weights or dried beans or rice so that the shells cannot bubble. Bake the shells in the preheated oven for 10 minutes. Remove the weights and foil and bake for another 10 minutes. Paint the shells with dijon mustard and bake for another 3 minutes, until the mustard has dried. Remove them from the oven and set aside.

To make the filling place the two cheeses in the workbowl of a food processor fitted with the metal blade. Turn the machine on and add the eggs one at a time. Scrape down the workbowl if necessary. Crush the saffron threads and add them to the cheese/egg mixture and blend well.

If you have time, chill the mixture before filling the shells. It will help prevent the filling from running over the shallow sides of the tart pans. You can make the filling two or three days in advance.

When ready to bake preheat the oven to 350°. Divide the filling between the two shells, using a rubber spatula to even out the filling and smooth the tops. Bake until the tarts just begin to puff and brown slightly, about 25 to 30 minutes. Cool on a rack.

After 20 minutes of cooling remove the sides of the tart pans and, with the aid of a long and thin-bladed spatula, gently slide the tart onto a large round serving platter. Serve slightly warm.

You may freeze the tart shells weeks in advance if you like and make the filling two or three days ahead, but it is not advisable to freeze the tart after baking.

K.T.

60 large mushrooms

1 lemon

4 to 6 tablespoons olive oil

3 tablespoons olive oil

1 large onion, diced

11 to 12 ounces Montrachet or other mild goat cheese, at room temperature

3 tablespoons freshly chopped herbs, such as thyme, dill and parsley

1/2 teaspoon kosher salt

Freshly ground black pepper, to taste

MUSHROOMS STUFFED WITH GOAT CHEESE AND HERBS

Clean the mushrooms by wiping gently with a slightly dampened paper towel. Remove the stems from the caps and reserve them. Using a melon baller remove the gills from the inside of the caps and discard.

If you are preparing the mushrooms ahead of time, toss the hollowed-out caps with some freshly squeezed lemon juice to preserve their color. Cover tightly and refrigerate. When you are ready to stuff the mushrooms pat them dry with paper towels.

Toss the caps with the 4 to 6 tablespoons of olive oil and reserve.

Dice the mushroom stems. In a sauté pan cook the onion in the olive oil over moderate heat until it is soft and translucent, about 3 to 4 minutes. Add the diced mushroom stems and cook until the liquid evaporates, about 3 minutes.

Add the goat cheese to the sauté pan and stir gently to combine. Be sure all the cheese melts. Remove the pan from the heat, add the fresh herbs, salt and pepper and taste and adjust the seasonings. Cool slightly.

Preheat the oven to 425°. Fill the mushroom caps with the cheese mixture and place in a single layer on an ungreased baking sheet.

Bake for 10 minutes, until the mushrooms are slightly browned and serve at once.

If you are stuffing the mushrooms in advance of baking, cover them and refrigerate for up to 6 hours. Bring to room temperature before baking.

DM

SHRIMP WITH GINGER AND CHILI PASTE

These make a fast-disappearing hors d'oeuvre or a generous first course for 6 to 8 persons.

1 1/2 pounds medium shrimp, shelled and deveined, tails left on

2 tablespoons vegetable oil

1 tablespoon dark-colored sesame oil

1 slice fresh ginger, minced

1 tablespoon soy sauce

1 tablespoon unseasoned rice vinegar or white wine vinegar

1 teaspoon chili paste (available in Oriental markets)

A few grinds black pepper

1 or 2 scallions, thinly sliced

Dry the shrimp well. Heat a very large sauté pan or wok over medium heat. Add the oils and ginger. As the ginger begins to sizzle move the pan on and off the heat so that it does not burn. Cook for about 2 minutes.

Raise the heat to high and add the shrimp. Cook, shaking the pan so the shrimp do not stick, until they are still slightly translucent in the middle but colored on the outside; this will take only a minute or two.

Add the soy, vinegar, chili paste and black pepper and cook until nearly all the moisture evaporates, moving the pan on and off the heat as necessary so the shrimp do not burn.

Slide the shrimp out of the pan onto a plate or platter. When cool enough to handle arrange them nicely on a serving tray. Sprinkle with some sliced scallion and serve at room temperature for best flavor. (If you like the shrimp even spicier toss them with a little more chili paste.)

DEVILED QUAIL EGGS

30 fresh quail eggs

3 tablespoons mayonnaise

2 tablespoons sour cream

1/2 teaspoon freshly squeezed lemon juice

3 ounces good quality lox, finely minced

1 tablespoon finely minced scallions

1/2 teaspoon kosher salt

Freshly ground black pepper, to taste

Pinch cayenne

Fresh quail eggs are frequently available in Japanese groceries. If unavailable you can use 12 chicken eggs as a substitute; they will not look quite as nice. Triple the amount of filling when using chicken eggs.

Place the quail eggs in a medium saucepan and fill with enough cold water to cover by 1 inch. Place over medium high heat and bring to a boil. Add a pinch of salt and simmer for 4 minutes (12 minutes for chicken eggs). Pour off the boiling water and add cold water to the pan until the eggs are cool.

Carefully peel the eggs and slice in half lengthwise. Use a sharp paring knife and wipe the blade after each cut so that the yolk does not remain on the blade. This will produce cleanly sliced egg halves. Reserve the egg halves in a single layer on a tray. Gently remove the yolk from each egg and place in a fine strainer set over a medium bowl. Using a rubber spatula press the yolk through the strainer into the bowl. To this add the rest of the ingredients except the egg whites. Combine thoroughly. Taste and adjust seasonings.

The easiest way to fill the eggs is with a pastry bag and a #4 pastry tube. (I suggest using a coupler attachment for the tube so that you can remove it easily and substitute another tip if necessary.) If you do not have a pastry bag you can spoon the mixture into the egg white halves using a small spoon.
Serve immediately or refrigerate, lightly covered, until ready to serve. Remove them from the refrigerator 30 minutes before serving so that they are only slightly chilled.

CRUST

2 cups all purpose unbleached flour

4 tablespoons cornmeal

1 teaspoon chili powder

2/3 cup well-chilled bacon fat, cut in pieces

6 to 8 tablespoons ice water

FILLING

2 large sweet red peppers

1/2 teaspoon chili powder

1 tablespoon olive oil

1/2 teaspoon lemon juice

TOPPING

6 tablespoons (3 ounces) unsalted butter

3 ounces cream cheese

1/4 pound shredded smoked cheese

2 tablespoons freshly chopped chives or green scallion tops

1 cup bread crumbs

1 tablespoon canned jalapeño chilies, chopped

1/4 teaspoon ground cumin

2 tablespoons chopped fresh parsley

6 ounces bacon, cooked crisply, drained (save the fat) and crumbled

2 egg whites

MEXICAN-STYLE RED PEPPER TARTS WITH CORNMEAL CRUST

This is my adaptation of a wonderful recipe developed by Betty Shenberger for a party for our cooking school assistants. The crust can be frozen well in advance of baking; the red pepper sauce can be made a couple of days in advance; and since these reheat so well I would advise that you actually bake them 1 day in advance of serving. It is a good idea to cook the bacon before making the crust so that you have the fat. Butter or a solid vegetable shortening can be used, but the flavor is just not the same.

To make the crust place the flour and cornmeal in the workbowl of a food processor fitted with the metal blade. Add the chili powder and pulse a couple of times to mix. Add the bacon fat and pulse until the mixture resembles coarse meal. With the machine running, pour the water in (taking about 5 to 10 seconds) and run until the dough just *thinks* about gathering together.

Press the dough into the bottom and up the sides of about 36 tiny muffin cups (often known as "gem pans"). Preheat the oven to 400º. (The crusts can be frozen at this point.) Bake the tart shells until they are set and slightly brown, about 10 to 12 minutes. Remove from the oven and cool to room temperature while preparing the filling.

To make the filling, char the sweet red peppers over a gas flame or directly on an electric burner set on high until the skin is blackened. Place in a plastic bag for 10 to 15 minutes to "steam," then scrape off the skin under running water. Remove the stem and seeds and purée in a food processor along with the chili powder, olive oil and lemon juice. Reserve.

To make the topping, melt the butter, cream cheese and smoked cheese together in a saucepan. Add the remaining ingredients except for the egg whites. Combine, then cool slightly. Beat the egg whites until stiff but not dry, then fold them into the cheese mixture.

To assemble the tarts, divide the red pepper purée among the baked shells and top with the cheese/bacon mixture. Bake in a 425º oven until the topping is set, about 15 minutes. Cool 5 minutes, then remove from the pans. Cool on a rack or serve warm.

K. T.

Ingredients

2 sticks (8 ounces) unsalted butter, at room temperature

1 1/2 cups sugar

Rind of one lemon, finely chopped

5 extra large eggs, separated

3 cups all purpose unbleached flour

1 tablespoon baking powder

3/4 cup milk

A coin wrapped in foil

1/2 to 1 cup whole, blanched almonds

Powdered sugar

VASILOPETA--ST. BASIL'S CAKE

This is a New Year's cake because in Greece St. Basil's Day is on January 1. The majority of Vasilopetas are made with yeast, much like the Tsourekia recipe in this book. The women in my husband's family always made this version, which is much like a pound cake. There is a coin hidden in the dough before baking, and almonds are used to form a cross and the year on the top of the cake. Traditionally, the cake is cut at midnight or the following day; the first piece is for Christ, the second for St. Basil, and the remainder for the master and mistress of the house and the guests in their turn. Whoever finds the baked-in coin in his or her piece will have good luck all the year. Chronia polla!!! Many years!!!!

Preheat the oven to 350º. Butter and flour a 12-inch round cake pan.

Cream the butter until it turns white. Add the sugar gradually and beat it until it is fluffy. Add the lemon rind, then the egg yolks one at a time. Beat until the last yolk is well-incorporated.

Stir together the flour and baking powder. Add a third of the flour mixture, then a third of the milk to the butter-sugar-egg mixture above, and continue mixing until all is used. Scrape the bowl frequently so that all of the flour is incorporated.

Beat the eggs whites until they are stiff but not dry. Carefully fold them into the batter with a large rubber spatula.

Scrape the batter into the buttered and floured cake pan, spreading it evenly. Press the coin into the batter so that it is completely covered. Lightly press the almonds into the top of the batter to represent a cross in the middle and the year on both sides of the cross.

Bake in the preheated oven until the center of the cake springs back when pressed lightly, about 40 to 45 minutes. A cake tester should come out clean.

Allow the cake to cool in the pan for 15 minutes. Carefully turn it out onto a rack. Place another rack on top of the cake and turn the cake over so the almond design is once again on top. Cool completely. To serve, place on a paper doily on a silver or crystal plate and dust the top of the cake with powdered sugar.

ALTERNATE MENU SUGGESTIONS

◆

FALL LUNCHEON

Watercress, Sweet Red Pepper and Cucumber Salad
French Rolls

Saffron Cheese Tart

Frozen Pear Cream; Candied Oranges dipped in Chocolate

◆

SAVORY BRUNCH

Cold Beet Soup

Pizza Jeannette
Asparagus with Kasseri

Chocolate Pecan Ring Loaf
Apples in Muscatel

◆

SPRING LUNCHEON

Pea Soup with Basil

Assorted Tea Sandwiches   Deviled Eggs*

Chocolate Ginger Angel Food Cake
in Rhubarb Sauce

* using Deviled Quail Egg recipe

◆

WINTER

East-West Chinese Black Mushroom Soup

Tournedos Taggart
Fagiolini al Burro

Sicilian Cassata

SPRING

Asparagus Salad with Pine Nuts

Curried Shrimp over Spaghetti

Ginger Ice Cream; Caramel Brownies

◆

Grilled Polenta with Olives and Red Peppers

Sautéed Chicken with Tarragon and Lime
Baby Carrots with Herbs

Coconut Cake

◆

SUMMER

Salad with Lemon Vinaigrette

Chicken Terrine with Curried Mayonnaise
Whole Wheat Sandwich Loaf

Fresh Strawberries with Balsamic Vinegar

◆

FALL

Salad Vinaigrette with Wild Mushrooms

Deep Dish Pizza

Poached Pears with White Wine and Ginger
Orange Custard Sauce

◆

Insalata Misticanza

Pepper and Almond Lasagne

Pear Tart Tatin

HEARTY DINNER FOR FRIENDS

Chilled Pumpkin Soup with Green Chilies

Border Pizza
Chili Pepper Pasta Salad

Sliced Papaya with Raspberry Sauce

◆

SIMPLY ELEGANT DINNER

Savory Mushroom Tart

Fillet of Red Snapper with Spicy Tomato Sauce

Salad with Lemon Vinaigrette

Fancy Yogurt in Chocolate Cups

◆

LIGHT COLD SUPPER

Caponata   French Bread

Insalata Composta

Spaghetti Squash Salad with Proscuitto

Individual Huckleberry Tarts

◆

DINNER FROM THE FAR EAST

Cold Tossed Sesame Noodles

Shrimp with Ginger and Chili Paste over Greens
Pilaf with Aromatic Spices
Dan's Barbecue Sauce with Pork Ribs

Fruites de Saison

◆

DINNER FOR THE BOSS

Salmon Rillettes
French Bread

Sauté of Pork with Rosemary Mustard Sauce
Pilaf with Aromatic Spices
Snow Peas with Shallots and Tarragon

Minty Yogurt Salad

Frozen Kir Sherbet

✦

COCKTAILS ONLY

Chicken Liver Paté   Rye Bread

Golden Savory Almonds

Kabob Mashwi

Feta Cookies

Savory Mushroom Tart

Crudités with Curried Mayonnaise

✦

DESSERT BUFFET

Cheesecake with Strawberry Sauce

Caramel Brownies

Sicilian Cassata

Chocolate Truffles

Fruites de Saison

Vasilopeta

✦